## Praise for *Outsiders*

'A powerful meditation on the relationship between race
and the natural world in modern Britain.'
*iNews*

'[*Outsiders*] is a bold step in confronting the
under-representation of people of colour in the natural
world, and helping those marginalised communities
to step forward to enjoy and protect it.'
*BBC Wildlife*

## Praise for Flock Together

'A birdwatching collective is not only encouraging people of
colour to explore green spaces, but to reconcile it with their
sense of identity.'
*The Telegraph*

'Inspiring young people to discover the wildlife on their
doorsteps.'
*The Times*

'During challenging times, what could be more rewarding?'
*Vogue*

T0008532

# Outsiders

# Outsiders

## Reclaim your place in nature

**OLLIE OLANIPEKUN AND NADEEM PERERA**

First published in Great Britain in 2022 by Gaia, an imprint of Octopus Publishing Group Ltd
Carmelite House
50 Victoria Embankment
London EC4Y 0DZ
www.octopusbooks.co.uk

An Hachette UK Company
www.hachette.co.uk

First published in paperback in 2023

ISBN 978-1-85675-481-1

A CIP catalogue record for this book is available from the British Library.

Printed and bound in the UK
10 9 8 7 6 5 4 3 2 1

Senior Commissioning Editor:
    Natalie Bradley
Senior Editor: Alex Stetter
Copy Editor: Jenny Wilson
Art Director: Mel Four
Typesetting: Jeremy Tilston at
    The Oak Studio Limited
Production Controller:
    Serena Savini

Illustrations: Olivia Twist
Line art on pp ii, vi, xii, 8, 38, 68, 100, 125, 126 and 156: Kyra Thompson

This FSC label means that materials used for the product have been responsibly sourced

MIX
Paper from responsible sources
FSC® C104740

For the Flock Together community, without whom none of this would be possible.

# PROLOGUE

## OLLIE

About ten years ago, I was at my brother's stag do, which was the usual affair – a group of us in the middle of a forest, quad biking, rafting and hiking...you know the score. At the end of the weekend, we were all loading onto the minibus ready to go home when I suddenly noticed an owl heading right towards me through the pine trees. In total silence, the owl and I shared this incredible moment and for a split second I'm sure I caught its eye. When I got home, I managed to find an old pair of binoculars at my parents' house, and from then on I was fascinated with birds.

I've been a naturalist for some years now, but I still have a lot to learn and am loving the journey that nature is taking me on. The outdoors is such an integral part of my life now that, after a few days without it, I almost get withdrawal symptoms and am itching to get back out there. Who knew that a stag do could be so life-changing?

A couple of years ago, I was posting some birdwatching pictures on my Instagram account when I noticed in the comments section that someone was naming all the species. I clicked onto the account and couldn't believe what I found: a young Black guy. I asked him, 'How do you know this stuff?' His reply: 'Man, I'm an avid birdwatcher.' It was such a serendipitous moment. I had always birdwatched on my own, with Google as my only companion. I had wanted to set up a birdwatching group for a while, and suddenly this expert birdwatcher was commenting on my posts. I just felt we had to do something together.

At the time, the world was on fire after the murder of George Floyd, and we were at the height of the Black Lives Matter movement. Many of us in the Black community were on our knees in despair about what was taking place. I always escape into nature when I feel this way, and it turned out that Nadeem did the same. With so many of our peers struggling and lacking support, we agreed to set up a birdwatching-turned-support club, for our community to gain the strength from nature that Nadeem and I had become so dependent on.

A couple of weeks later, we were getting ready for our first walk and met in person for the first time. Sat on a park bench, we spoke for hours, sharing stories about our background and what nature meant to us. Trying to think of a name for the club,

I told Nadeem that I had been playing with the word 'flock'. Straight away, he responded 'together', and so our community took flight.

Flock Together is an idea, a concept. It's been in the works our whole lives. The journeys we have taken were for this reason. We didn't know it then, but all along our lived experiences had been directing us to this moment. All the things you're about to read are the ingredients to that main course. It might appear on the surface that Flock Together just dropped out of the sky, but the reality is that it was formulated through histories, enduring resilience and the constant need to uplift our people.

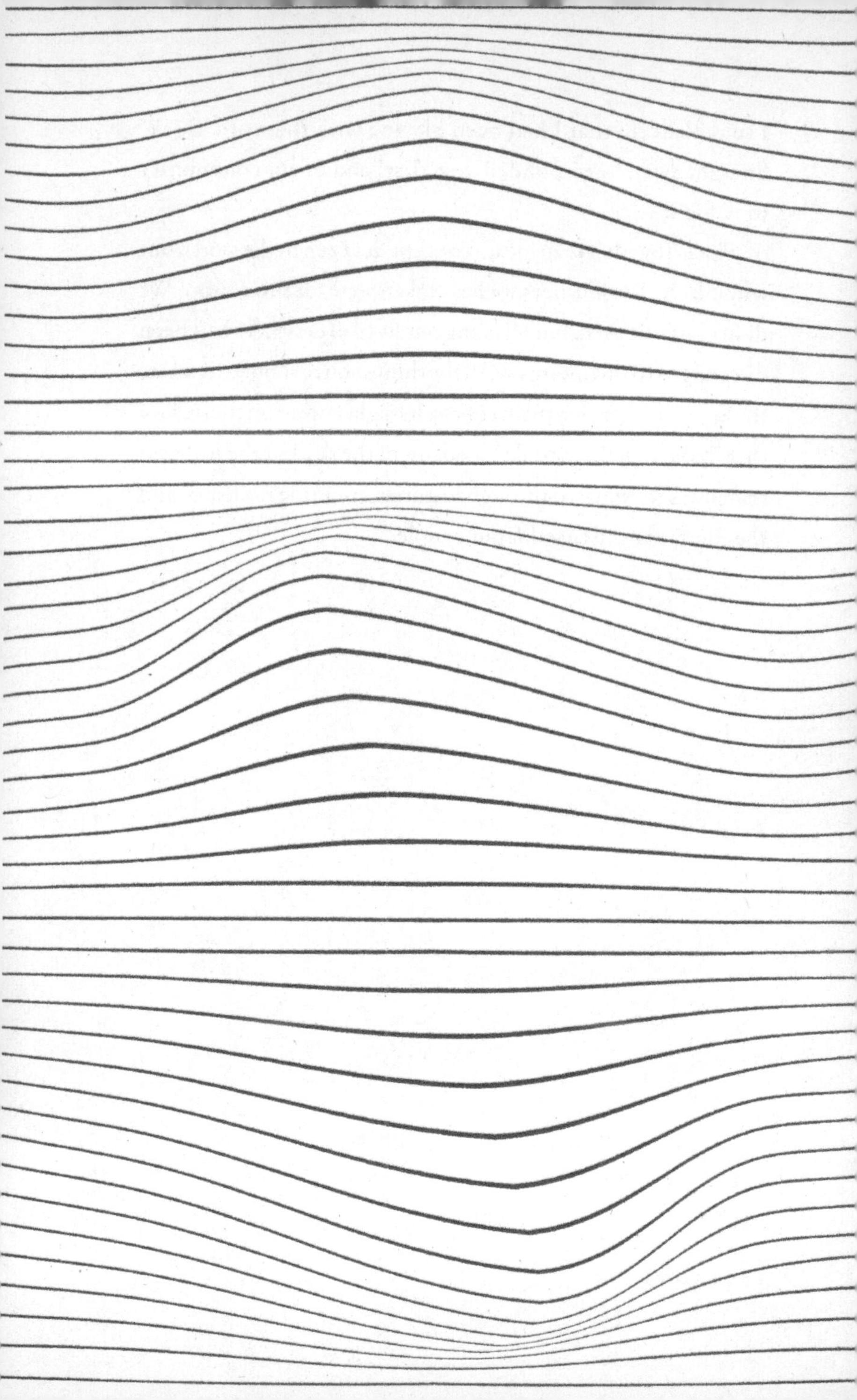

# INTRODUCTION

## OLLIE & NADEEM

The primary objective of Flock Together is to combat the under-representation of people of colour in the natural world. We set out to create a space where people of colour felt safe and supported within nature, but it quickly became apparent that we had so much more to offer. Neither of us was prepared for the reaction we received, but as soon as we launched our first walk, the response made us realize that this was answering a need within our community. From the start, it has been about so much more than birdwatching. Flock started with two people, a mutual love of nature and a shared vision, but soon became a cultural movement involving thousands of people, walks all over the world, TV and radio appearances, magazine covers, product releases, music releases and global brand partnerships. We were even recipients of a congratulatory letter from the UK prime minister.

We're here to make a difference, and we're here to do something that has never been done. But before anything else, we're here for the betterment of people of colour. We want to push the limit of imagination when it comes to the experience of our community. Yes, it's a birdwatching collective, but it's also a creative platform and an outdoors movement – that's the beauty of it. Choosing not to pigeonhole ourselves, we quickly knew we needed to be a fluid, dynamic and adaptable model that reflected our ever-growing global community, never limiting the places or spaces we can enter.

'Connecting with nature' is one of those phrases that risks being both ambiguous and clichéd, something thrown around that might not mean much to a lot of people. To truly connect, and to benefit from this experience like we have, you have to arrive at a stage where you see yourself as an inextricable part of nature. You are nature, and nature is you. The journey to this understanding is unique for everyone. We can't tell you how or expect what worked for us to work for you. But the crucial starting point is being open – don't let statements like 'nah, that's a white thing' get in the way.

We see a clear link between the plight of our people and the plight of nature, and how, by benefitting one, we can also benefit the other. Our stories align in many ways. We have both been abused and destroyed for the capitalistic gain of many nations, which continue to hold a degree of power over our current living conditions, and yet, despite this historical exploitation, we are still plentiful in energy, love and creativity. Our spirits can never be broken. We want to highlight the joys and true wonder of the natural world as a benefit to our community, but also emphasize the importance of giving back to nature in the way that it endlessly gives to us.

Through the collective, and now this book, we aim to inspire a new wave of naturalists and conservationists who will unify causes in a way that benefits communities and the natural world, with the understanding that they are both the same thing. Through the work we do and through the words in this book, we have many ambitions to inspire anybody, no matter your ethnicity, to re-evaluate your understanding of the world around you and to begin to blur the lines between nature and yourself. Understand that we are only divided by arbitrarily placed lines put in place to confuse and distract us from the fact that we, as people, are all one, and that that oneness also includes nature. The world that we are accustomed to relies on division and individualism; the world that we hope for is one of unification, mutualism, love and peace. Flock Together is necessary right now – for solidarity and awareness, and to help raise our people to parity – but we hope one day true equality and unity will be a reality.

To date, Flock Together has been a massively rewarding and eye-opening journey, which we are honoured to be a part of and to share with you all. We have experienced unfathomable highs, extreme lows, twists and all sorts of turns, each one ultimately preparing us for where we are today. This book is our story, both individual and collective. We want to share some of the experiences we have had to navigate as people of colour and the coping mechanisms we've used to overcome the challenges that have confronted us. Through sharing our stories of healing through nature, we hope to inspire you to approach the outdoors with an open heart and mind. That might sound like a vague and ineffectual statement, especially if your life hasn't been all rosy, but the outdoors really has guided us in defining, developing and nurturing both ourselves and our communities. Through this book we hope you, too, will be on your way to understanding that nature has endless benefits.

Since its conception, Flock Together has been growing fast. We have several thousand people on our mailing list and have been lucky enough to inspire many to fly the Flock flag in major cities all over the world. After only our first walk, we collaboratively established a set of pillars that would go on to serve as the direction in which Flock Together would operate. This process was a result of Ollie's understanding of how to make an idea work. His experience in creative problem-solving was coming good. Ollie saw just what his idea could do for our people and our connection to the planet. When he met Nadeem, he saw somebody who was thinking the same way. See here, the power of *ideas*. Together, aided by early and beloved group members, we agreed upon the pillars which would ensure that Flock Together could achieve positive results, not only for our community but for the nature that we inhabit too.

The following six chapters are aligned with Flock Together's original six pillars: *Benefits of Nature, Challenging Preconceptions, Mental Health Benefits, Building Community, Ecological Benefit* and *Creative Mentorship*. This said, we have always had to react, move and adapt to many situations on our journey. No two days are the same, and we are constantly questioning and revising just what these pillars mean as different situations present themselves to us. We assigned ourselves three pillars each, based on our areas of expertise and interests: Ollie, the OG, the innovator, the creative, at a very different stage in his journey from Nadeem, the football coach, the nature boy, the apprentice. Both of us share our contrasting personal stories to speak about important issues that we have faced as individuals, as a duo, and as part of a community.

In his chapters, Ollie explores the power of social media to share information and creative solutions, and brings the energy of the creative industry into the conversation around wildlife and nature conservation. Having built a handsome reputation for creating social impact, he offers insight into how the arts and culture aren't a world away from nature at all, and shares what it's like to be the brainpower behind one of the biggest cross-pollinators of two industries that our culture has ever seen.

Nadeem explores his personal story, detailing his account of growing up in East London, overcoming hardship and finding salvation in nature. Having been birding since he was a child, he offers the unique perspective of a boy from the hood who was breaking the mould for future generations, without even knowing it. He shares his hopes for the future of Flock Together and just how important it is for marginalized communities to take up space, not only as enjoyers of green spaces but also as protectors.

This book doesn't have all the answers for our community, but within it there are many stories that can serve as guidance for our peers and generations to come. We know that once younger generations take an interest in things, innovation is bound to follow...and the natural world, of all places, is in dire need of innovation. We are proud to share this book with you all, whether you are a person of colour or not, and even though Flock Together stands to fight against ideas that are unpleasant to think about, we, as an organization, are focused on nothing but bringing joy to our community, championing unheard voices and keeping our ambitions and targets lofty, creative and innovative!

# 1

# MAKE NATURE A MUST

## NADEEM

Living beings, not least human beings, are happiest when they are allowed to carry out their most true purpose. A quick and easy example of this is a study which showed that animals that roam huge territories in the wild – particularly large predators (the presence of which is a great indicator of a healthy, biodiverse ecosystem) – show far higher levels of stress and psychological scarring in captivity than those animals that don't need as much space.[1]

An organism and its behaviour over time become shaped by and almost indistinguishable (or inseparable) from the environment the organism inhabits. Its behaviour, then, is not the result of an innate set of instructions conceived at the same time as the organism itself. It is more accurate to say that the behaviour of any being is a window into the history of an organism. Each action of any animal tells a story of what its ancestors had to overcome and how they had to adapt in order to survive. A living organism itself is a set of genetic clues, building up a picture for a wider historical context. So, if a person (or animal) is not allowed to live out their desired function, it is understandable that this being should sink into pits of depression, feelings of uselessness and other undesirable outcomes.

Case in point: I was coming off the back of an unsuccessful schooling and my relationship with my family was tethered by a weakening rope. My desires to be understood by the people around me and my environment left me with a chip on my shoulder when I realized that these desires could not be met. There was no space for my being to exist as it was. I was constantly told that I had to chop, change and edit myself in order to find my place in this world; a concept I still struggle with at twenty-eight years old.

This realization, along with long-standing childhood trauma, meant that I would carry what I then described as a 'huge sack of sadness' around with me on a daily basis. The sack itself was painful enough to acknowledge; however, carrying it around every day became tiresome. The more tired I became, the heavier it felt. This sack and its associated burdens left me feeling further saddened, alienated and unloved. I wanted help, but mental fatigue and great pain saw me swinging the sack wildly at those who tried to come near enough to assist, and I guess society just didn't have the patience or enough concern to understand that. So, I suffered, often alone and in tears.

It was nature that would prove to be my saving grace and the kickstarter of my journey towards self-realization and, ultimately, a happier life. My lifestyle up until that point might not have been intrinsically linked to the natural world, but at twenty years old, when I was struggling with my sack of sadness, I started to spend a considerable amount of my time cycling through my home city of London, using its bicycle-hire scheme. I enjoyed exposing myself to all that the city had to offer and, moreover, the parts with which I was greatly unfamiliar. A day came when I was exploring Google Maps and stumbled upon a massive green space on the opposite side of London to me. This green space was called Richmond Park and, though I didn't realize it at the time, it was due to change the course of my life.

After discovering the whereabouts of Richmond Park, I decided to make the 90+ minute train journey to see what I felt had been a secret before then (the location was beyond the scope of the hired bike docking stations, so I had to take the train). Of course, Google Maps is free for all to use, but this park, or any green space for that matter, had never been mentioned to me before. I had been to parks on the odd occasion, but nobody around me really spoke about recreational grounds or woods. So there I was, a young Black man futilely gripping my adolescence, trying to find my place in the world, and hoping to do so in a spot I had never visited before and was all too unfamiliar with.

Richmond Park's host borough, Richmond upon Thames, is in the top three London boroughs for lowest crime rates, has been described as the greenest borough in the capital and also ranks in the top three boroughs, out of thirty-two, for state schooling. From Richmond station I would walk the twenty minutes through the district to reach the park and on my way I saw nothing but affluence. *My* home borough, Newham, on the other hand, sits solidly in the top three for the greatest number of violent crimes in London, as well as having its highest rates of poverty. In 'my ends', as we call it, I would see bookies, off-licences, crackheads and cheap fried chicken shops. In Richmond, I was seeing cafés, bookshops and a branch of Waitrose supermarket (still a few crackheads, though). At the time, everything in Richmond looked, frankly, better.

A particularly relevant standout for me was the Richmond Hill viewpoint. This sits above the River Thames just across the road from my favourite pub in the area, the Roebuck. It is situated on Richmond Hill (also the name of the street), which takes you into the park via the Richmond Gate. The view from the hill is *the only English view protected by an Act of Parliament*. Must be important. The viewpoint also features the Terrace Gardens, a public space open for all to enjoy (or certainly all who know it exists). On a summer's day, locals can visit the pub from atop the hill, bask in luscious and lofty views of the Thames cutting through vast stretches of uninterrupted green, and breathe in some noticeably fresh air. These views can provide a great platform for reflection and thoughts of empowerment, foresight, peacefulness and perspective. Such is the nature of greenery and sitting or standing safely at an elevated position. An individual is likely to feel more important and capable simply because they are able to see all that surrounds them, as opposed to having their view impaired and obstructed. As the body does, so the mind follows.

I grew up in the Docklands, also just a stone's throw from the Thames. On the bank opposite me was the O2 Arena, the famous venue. For those unfamiliar with East London's docklands, its history boasts a massive role in London's trade, particularly in times of hardship, having survived the bombings of the Second World War and the economic downturn during the 1970s and '80s. The area was a global trading hub and essential to London's overseas industry from the late 1700s. This, however, meant that the space in the immediate vicinity of the river was not accessible to the public, provided no glimpses of any greenery and certainly didn't have a view protected by Parliament.

Instead, to this day there are fences, barbed wire, piles of scrap and rubbish, and towering chimneys that bellow ominous smoke all day long. These relics of capitalism do not inspire feelings of empowerment and capability, but rather remind the local public that there are places they simply cannot access without submitting themselves to the rules of a game they had no part in designing; not to mention, witnessing first-hand the pollution entering their living space. The benefits of nature had been deliberately removed from the public so as to better enforce their servitude and dull their spirits – the opposite to the treatment of Richmond residents.

Here we have a river that, in accordance with rigorous social engineering, can be presented either as a depressing, soul-sucking part of a landscape or as a haven that provides great relaxation and inspiration. The activity in the docklands exploits those who work tirelessly to feed themselves and find their daily security, only able to dream of living in Richmond (if they know it exists) or of doing anything about the state of the place in which they live. The grass is literally greener on the other side (of the river). And, worse still, it is so by design.

I made a habit of soaking up the vibes of the haven which had been placed far from my reach. Were it not for this moment of innovation in my behaviour, I would never have been able to witness some of the most incredible and intimate moments that a country has to offer; moments which very few can say that they have had the pleasure of observing, despite them being totally free to access. Moments evoke feelings, and feelings inform our decision-making. We should all be aiming to enjoy the fruitful buffet of moments that the natural world has to offer in abundance. Devour each enjoyable moment with delight and do not fret in the pursuit of new thoughts.

It was from the Richmond Hill viewpoint, while enjoying England's only protected view, that the penny dropped. I deserved to be in Richmond, even if nobody in Richmond agreed. Once I entered the park gates, none of them existed anyway. And so, for the next two years, I would visit that park at least two or three times a week, staying easily for eight hours at a time. Its size, at over 2,500 acres (a football pitch is less than 2 acres), means you can get lost for a little bit if you're not careful, which, funnily enough, is a rather liberating feeling. The Western human being today has become so accustomed to knowing where they are and where they should be at all times that they risk losing something called *instinct*, a necessary tool in the art and activity of birding.

To be lost in exploration is a fundamental human attribute which makes us stronger; being 'lost' isn't a bad thing! Being lost is, in fact, a fantastic way to explore the world around you, and thus explore who it is that you are. If you are constantly acting in situations with secure and likely outcomes, how much of your being has been designed by you and how much has been crafted by a system? If you are reliably in the same place, carrying out the same tasks, day in and day out, you are more like a machine than a true human being. Of course, this is necessary to do sometimes, but I really don't think that it's what being human is all about.

A particular moment of being lost once brought me a great surprise. It was the moment I saw a kestrel (*Falco tinnunculus*) hovering in place in the air. It was suspended beautifully against the backdrop of Richmond Park. This bird was one half of a breeding pair, which had made a particular patch of the park their regular hunting grounds. I could reliably find them on my visits and they were an easy bird for me to identify, having seen them on the A13 dual carriageway on almost every journey I would take in my mum's car when I was a child.

As a kid, I thought the kestrel I saw from the car was an eagle because I could recognize the features of a bird of prey. I learned with age that a kestrel is indeed a species of falcon, but every bit as interesting as any eagle. For one, they have an incredible ability to fly into oncoming wind at the exact same speed as the wind that is hitting them. This makes them look like they are stuck in place, and is an easy way to identify them.

All birds of prey are specialized to hunt and kill in order to survive. This sounds brutal, but it provides a massive service to the ecosystem. It's also often the entry point for young and excitable bird lovers. In the UK, there are mainly two types of vole a kestrel will find for dinner: the field vole (*Microtus agrestis*) and the bank vole (*Myodes glareolus*). For those who don't know, voles are just like mice but with shorter tails; they love open spaces far more than their longer-tailed counterparts who are thigmophilic (love to make contact with surfaces). If kestrels *weren't* hunting voles, then grass would soon disappear. Grasses compose much of the vole's diet and, without a predator controlling vole numbers, grasses and other vegetation would suffer massively. There would eventually reach a point whereby the grass becomes insufficient to sustain the vole population and the voles themselves would then die out. So, try your best not to be all human about it; death is necessary to sustain life.

I had become pretty well practised in finding the kestrels on my visits to Richmond. Not because kestrels are robot-like and can be found in the same place day in and day out, but because the order of nature sees that species rest delicately upon one another in a lifelong relationship of feeding and sustaining, with none benefitting unfairly from a situation or exploiting the other in the name of expansion. There is no need to leave a place if it gives you as much as you give *it*.

One of my favourite things about birding is looking at a snapshot of the landscape. In this case, an open meadow lined with trees. Once I have this snapshot, the wildlife to be found there can be filled in by imagination. An open field means voles; voles mean kestrels, tawny owls (*Strix aluco*) and countless other predators. Each species infers a number of reasons for the budding naturalist to become excited. The beauty of nature is that the presence of one species (particularly predators) implies the existence of several others, so no one creature exists as a standalone organism to rule over its neighbours. Each one is a note thoughtfully placed on the sheet music from which all the natural world plays. This is the opposite of our flawed existence as capitalist human beings, where seeing somebody with lots of money implies the exploitation of and distancing from others, many of whom will never be as fortunate.

I once spotted the male kestrel take a vole up into a tree. I could have gone home happy with this because it was indeed the first time that I had witnessed a kestrel hunting. However, because of my honed instincts (acquired through having the freedom to explore), I kept watching and I was able to see an aspect of behaviour that really put the cherry on top of my warm London evening of a sundae. As soon as you enter the park, you are most likely to hear two calls: the 'kek-kek-kek-kek-kek-kek' of the ring-necked parakeet (*Psittacula krameri*) and the relatively subdued 'kaaw, kaaw, kaaw' of the jackdaw (*Coloeus monedula*). It was the jackdaw this time that would make a surprise appearance as two of them swooped in from nowhere and began to attack the kestrel. Kestrels aren't particularly powerful birds and the male is usually smaller than the female, so the male I was watching was unable to put up much of a fight against the crafty members of the crow family (*Corvidae*). Forced to abandon its kill, the kestrel fled and

left the vole to be enjoyed by the jackdaws. It was one of my first insights into the true genius of the corvid (crow) family of birds, who would have sat and watched the kestrel hunt its prey before they made their move. They have since become my favourite birds to watch. This memory stuck with me because it was one of the first times that I managed to get a view of some intriguing animal behaviour, which would have gone completely unseen by the human eye had I not taken the initiative to visit this park across the city from me. Get outside, guys!

Richmond Park would provide me with countless wildlife experiences. I fell in love with that green space and it continues, to this day, to be my favourite place in London. I love the park not only because of its sheer size but also because it allows me to get back to the very basics of what it means to be a human being: getting outside and exploring the world with no other motivation than to explore the way you currently feel. This is an ancient wisdom that children carry, and indeed a wisdom which we take away from ourselves as we turn into adults.

This freedom to explore that I found in Richmond Park can properly be found anywhere. I find myself inspired by any journey I take into unfamiliar parts of not only rural England but also pockets of urban settings that the privileged have claimed for their own.

Growing up, I very much enjoyed exploring and wandering with no real destination in mind. There was always an air of adventure about my endeavours. My mum would tell me that night-time was for sleeping. At that time – and the same is often true even now – I couldn't help but wonder what happened in the world during this strange dark period with no sun and no people. Were the pavements all empty? Who was driving cars around when they should be in bed? Were they allowed to do that? Can I do that? This is a very typical and natural perspective for the human child – that is, to be generally inquisitive and fuelled by a sense of wonder and exploration.

As children, we use our senses to their fullest extent, following our noses, eyes, hands, ears and most importantly, our hearts. Smell, sight, touch and sound are all resultant from external stimuli that evoke our reactions – involuntarily, in most cases. Perhaps we have a slightly better control of our sense of touch, but it is really only our sense of taste that will almost always be stimulated voluntarily by ourselves. We are born as blank canvases, seeking to become filled with character, colour and stories! To be able to live and follow these instincts is not just the single most precious gift given to us by the phenomenon of life but it is the ability most easily taken away from us as we grow upward in order to meet the demands of the world around us. These are demands which nature does not make.

I think this is important in understanding human beings and the role we are to play in the world. We are liable to adopt ways of thinking through a code fed to us by experiences. As people in the modern world, we will undoubtedly find ourselves subject to forced layers of identity. This is to say that, to some degree, any individual is likely to gain a sense of self from the world's reaction to them, so then that gradually established self may be composed of characteristics and qualities acquired through unwanted yet unavoidable experiences. This can happen subtly through experiences that are imposed on a person, as opposed to them building their own character through the fruitful experience of willing exploration.

A person of African origin (a term used synonymously by me with 'Black'), particularly such a person in the Western world, is often subject to astounding levels of racism, and it would be within reason to say that this happens on a daily basis. You can imagine the effects of this on a person's self-perception – something I would like to explore here, as well as how we can offset this through exposure to nature. It is important to acknowledge that, contrary to the belief of many white people I have spoken with, I deem it totally irrational for a person of non-European descent to identify with their European country of birth ahead of the culture to which they owe their physical body. Now, before I carry on, I will provide my validity to align my experiences with that of a person of African origin. While it is true that I was raised by my Sri Lankan family and am, in terms of my home life, a Sinhala Buddhist Sri Lankan, my father is a Jamaican man. I have gained my sense of identity, in part, by observing how I am treated. I am treated by wider British society as a Black man. This chapter contains examples of such treatment.

In my early twenties, having now discovered my little haven in Richmond, I found myself working in hospitality, in an attempt to build a life for myself. I was a barman in an English pub. At over four hundred years old, the pub predated the majority of others in London. It is named The Mayflower and is a proud historical landmark in the South London riverside community of Rotherhithe. The pub is named after the first vessel to sail from England, in 1620, to a 'new Promised Land' (what is America today). On that ship were the first European colonists of New England. I was angered to learn of the history of the ship as I began to work at the pub. I had never learned about it at school, and yet the captain of the ship was from the same part of the world as me. While the *Mayflower* itself did not harbour any brutally enslaved African people, the pilgrims aboard soon established their settlement in Plymouth, Massachusetts, as part of the expansion of the British colonies in America, to which the use of enslaved Africans was crucial. The history of the *Mayflower* was selectively excluded from the school curriculum despite having a huge significance to my individual history, as well as the history of my community. Not having it taught to me and learning about it later, by chance, caused me anguish. Such is the nature of environments and their effects on those who inhabit them. My history had been shrouded by a culture and people who did not invite me to share their space. Why all the secrecy? The effect was for me to feel that I was treated with contempt by omission. To me, the blue plaque on the pub was a badge of (dis)honour that was brandished proudly above the bodies and labour of my ancestors, and it was now hanging over my soul. Nonetheless, I was made to overlook this traumatizing history because I urgently needed the job at the time.

The reality is that it is usually a highly favoured person

who is able to make something that matters a viable means of employment. The way in which we exist in London (and I'd guess it's the same for any major city or town in what is regarded as the 'Western world') is often a way of contradiction. We, particularly as people of colour, may fundamentally disagree with most of the things that shape our daily lives and yet, by our daily actions, most of us live as hypocrites. We, as human beings and people of colour, certainly, morally, do not support many of the ideas which our actions seem to prop up, either directly or indirectly, but we, being forced by our living conditions, must contradict our innate moral standings and overlook the questionable ethics of our decisions on a frequent basis.

By way of necessity, for most of us, the problems of the world must take lower priority to the problems of our daily lives as individuals. This is the predicament faced by the human being in the modern day, or certainly, at least, by the Westerner who is subject to barrages of propaganda on a daily basis. A very simple example shows itself in the amount of time we spend acknowledging the number of people across the globe without food and the amount of time we could spend trying to help them. This time is instead used in pursuit of feeding ourselves because, for most of us reading this, our own individual guarantee of food on our respective tables hangs by a precarious thread. See here the slow and precise severing of the global community and the individual.

If we were to consider exactly what we wish to do with our working time – that is to say, most of our time – our discussion could open up here. What does a dream job look like, or even mean? Do we know ourselves well enough to know what we *actually* want? Is the thing currently taking up most of our time related to what we really want at all? When inspected just a little closer, all of these questions come down to one fundamental thing: human beings acquire a sense of self by interacting with their environment and the people around them. We want to be fulfilled. After all, how would you know what you'd like to do if you had no environment to try things out? If what we like depends on who we are, then who are we? Is *who we are* a perception, slowly built over time, moment by moment, in a constant dance of interactions with environments and people, like rain shaping mountains?

How much can a child be affected by the environment in which they find themselves? What would become of a child with a genius level of intelligence if they were only ever exposed to disastrous conditions? What are the chances that that child would be able to direct themselves onto a fruitful and sustainable path? How much would those chances be hindered by growing up in a harmful environment? How many children could a harmful environment claim if the environment was left neglected and allowed to fester, becoming firmer in its place in the world? It is my sound belief that if we were allowed (or if we allowed ourselves) to ponder and reflect on these questions to their fullest extents, then nobody would be able to commit themselves to a nine-to-five job, which only perpetuates and exacerbates the overbearing issues which begin to expose themselves. These would be issues regarding inequality, corruption and nepotism; the lack of community, fulfilment and love; and the existence of senseless and unjustified violence, both blatant and subtle.

These issues do not arise in nature. This is far from the way the world came to become the beautiful cradle which sustains us now. After realizing these things in detail, I believe that we, the people, would seek resolution of our issues through productive means and methods of collaboration with people of similar thinking and needs. Our working life is unavoidable; fine. Let's say that we accept this notion. Is it right, then, that the benefit of our work goes almost entirely to a select and highly favoured few and not to those within society who have been left in a dark cave with no lamp and no directions, but expectations that we will find our own way out? What is the time that we spend working at our jobs costing these neglected and lost pockets of our society? We have only a finite amount of time after all.

If we ourselves have mouths to feed, rotas to follow, deadlines to meet and bosses to take orders from, there is very little, if any, time left to do things that matter. 'Things that matter' is a term which here relates to the issue of environments and their people being neglected by those who are supposed to be responsible for their collective wellbeing. If the gardener has to do housework in order to keep their garden, then who will tend the garden? How long will the gardener spend in the house before they find themselves staring at the garden through the window, forgetting what the grass beneath their feet feels like? If a person is in an environment that resembles the aforementioned 'cave', then, in the real world, this means that they have little to no opportunity for progression in their lives. This is due to social engineering. The affected people will be far more likely to adopt undesirable ways of behaviour through the subtle coercion of their immediate surroundings.

My life in hospitality provided me with several incredibly profound and insightful experiences. Having lived a life reasonably isolated from 'mainstream society' before my first bar job, I had very little understanding of my place in the world, and moreover the space I thought to be accessible to me. One such experience was not just an isolated incident but rather a repeated phenomenon which constantly reminded me, in small conditioning doses, of how I was perceived and thus reinforced a continual re-imaging of how I ought to think of myself. After all, our perception of ourselves is probably the most valuable one, but it is really others' perceptions of us, as individuals, which will have the most tangible impact on our lives, should we wish to integrate and progress through society.

I would spend a great portion of any pub shift clearing away empty plates and glasses. This, of course, meant that I would have to approach tables and ask if the seated party were happy with the food they had and if they would like anything to be taken away (great waiter, I am). More often than not, I would approach the table and before I could even utter a single word, a member of the party (usually a white woman) would immediately grab their phone which had been lying on the table totally unguarded beforehand. This is ridiculous, firstly, because I would have easily been able to swipe any phone left on any table as I patrolled the dining spaces looking for plates to clear. I certainly wouldn't draw the attention of the entire table before attempting to steal a phone which would be subsequently blocked by the network provider and become totally useless and of very little value to anyone. My criminal expertise unfortunately extends only so far. On a more serious note, this knee-jerk reaction from my white counterparts revealed a long-standing and deeply rooted perspective of the white experience...which might not be as sinister as it initially seems.

I was constantly reminded that I was not welcome and, no matter how friendly I pretended to be for the sake of my job, I would almost always be suspected of having a criminal motive for my actions. We can explore from where this preconception derives in another chapter (see page 39). To be suspected of being a phone thief while doing your job is painful enough in itself, but when I reflected further, I was able to understand a little bit more about the situation. It is important to reflect on situations past; sometimes it is like reliving a moment through the eyes of another person. The recalled moments tend to take a less manipulated, more objective, shape and this is helpful in drawing lessons from your experience. In this instance, reflection brought me to the realization that, in what I thought to be my environment, I was not free to exist as a human being. In the eyes of my neighbours, I simply could not exist independently of a preconceived set of ideas. The ideas in question are rooted in a meticulous erasure of history and the liberal use of violence to impose, on people of African origin, a false image and then, by sharing this false image with the rest of the world, to reinforce the idea. This course of action provides a predetermined context for the African to exist in; one which is mostly unfavourable to them. My reflections also allowed me to recognize my masculinity and to realize that, to a woman of any ethnic background, that has its own implications because of the experiences that women have within this terribly broken society.

It takes no genius to figure out that to be perceived as a criminal before being known as an individual is an unfavourable position to be in and, if this phenomenon is widespread and repeated, that it will have a massive effect on the initial interaction between two people. This becomes hugely significant when it is considered that, historically speaking, a person of African descent, particularly those who arrived in the West as brutally enslaved people, is naturally and understandably more likely to begin life in a place, in Western society, far below any of their white counterparts. That is not to say that there aren't white people who begin in unfavourable positions, but rather that, proportionally, the numbers will vary greatly between the two groups.

Africans were ripped from their land, their languages, their food, their history, their spiritual beliefs and their communities, having grown to know only these things. They were then brutalized for centuries by deplorable means and regarded as subhuman. After the Europeans had had their fill, the people of African descent were given their 'freedom', often with very little infrastructure to support them once they were 'free'. Many Africans then find themselves in the Western world, searching for a place to thrive: a loving, healing and safe space. But it is the social engineering of the European which does not facilitate this, nor does it care to. That's why it is crucial that we build our own safe spaces.

When this wider context is given and understood, we can see that it is not the African who ought to have a negative preconception about themselves spread about through mainstream media (for example, popular Black British films like *Kidulthood* and *Blue Story* that are centred on gang culture) but rather the European. Ignoring this, even, it should be the African who is afforded opportunities in the understanding that they are far further from a secure position in society than a European, not only because of the brutality and historic handicaps they have faced through European social engineering, but also because the effect of these things causes them to fall far behind in the race of capitalism. Irretrievably so, in some cases, with families cursed by drug addictions and cycles of violence, often against a backdrop of poverty, poor mental health and public disinterest. The person of African descent, in the Western world, is constantly fighting an uphill battle to break down the preconceptions laid out in front of them, all for the sake of being able to be understood and accepted as an equal. This shows us that Africans and Europeans exist in a dynamic of great inequality in daily Western life.

I would here like to be excused, by some of my own community, for having to highlight the problems we face. I am aware that many of us are already well versed in this area of discussion and have long been busying ourselves with seeking solutions. However, I am constantly astounded by the total lack of understanding of my story and, in turn, the story of my community, that I encounter, though this lack of understanding is something I am all too familiar with. There may therefore be some Westerners who need bringing up to speed, and I would also like to highlight issues for young people of my community.

All of this considered, if we accept that a *part* of my *true desire* is to explore and adventure, then I can say that the desire was somewhat met by my life as a pint-pouring, nocturnal grafter. I became incredibly familiar with London's streets, having had to travel home to East London, from all four corners of its map, at what were usually ungodly hours. It felt as though my inner explorer was being satisfied because exploring, paired with meeting financial and social obligations, met most of my practical needs at the time, although leaving me with little time for inspiration, relaxation or perspective. I had succumbed to the trap. I was forgoing my time fighting for things that *matter* in order to pay my rent and feed myself, which was doubly hard, seeing that the money I was earning per hour at the time was barely enough to cover these ever-present necessities of life. This is the cruel engineered effect of minimum wage employment. I was earning very little money and spending more than half my monthly income on my rent, which is still, of course, a better prospect than being homeless. This is an incredibly worrying pathway to resolve; however, it is the condition of living in a major conurbation like London.

There came a time at which, while being partially satisfied by my job as a barman, I realized that I was not being totally fulfilled; another, prioritized, true desire was still in great need of being met. This is to show that *true desires* exist in multiples and also in varying orders of priority. True desires are innate in all of us, but can easily be stifled and lost by *what* and, more importantly, *who* we learn to be while living in our respective environments.

The time had come for me to dig deep and satisfy my inner child, but to try to find security along the way. But who was this inner child? I had learned, from my urban environment, so many things; some useful and some not so much. But all the things I had learned, no matter how useless or useful, caused me to unlearn my instinctive exploration. This was very different from the natural world and from birding itself, which are all about following your instincts.

Experiences speak in ways that our subconscious (soul) can understand. Language, on the other hand, speaks to us in a way that our *conscious mind* can understand. It was my soul that urged me to seek out Richmond Park without knowing a good reason for it. It was my conscious mind that decided to stay once it saw good reason. We enjoy great spectacles, amazing flavours and sweet music because these moments evoke feelings within us that can influence our mood and decision-making. Nature can always provide us with all these things at zero cost. It is, then, important to examine how particular experiences become more likely (and unlikely) to befall an individual, how the incidental conflict between some of the likely experiences and the true desires of an individual play out, and finally how nature facilitates the true desire (or certainly the exploration of it) of human beings and indeed all life.

I realize now that I was made to be outdoors. My body is composed of genetics from two tropical islands. My ancestors will have had far more days where they didn't need shelter than when they did. They were probably accustomed to tropical birdsong accompanying them on treks through jungle, plucking fruits from trees, feeling dirt beneath their feet, and generally living in perfect harmony with the land, flora and fauna surrounding them. They probably had no need to sit inside caves for most of the year to hide from blizzards and concoct desperate and awful plans and theories about the world.

With that being said, what can we, as a community of non-European people, do to offset the harmful effects of our environment? Nature is the answer! Find your own Richmond Park! Whether European, Asian, African, Latin American or from the lost city of Atlantis, we have all come from nature and historically have lived in a delicate symbiosis between our people, the native wildlife and the nature of the land. This is where we can begin to find our true identity and then our desires.

Do not fear the masses of snooty, middle- to upper-class white people turning their noses up at you when you walk their streets. Do not pay any attention to their minds which are starved of compassion and love. Walk through their streets and find the park they all wish you never to find. If you are uncomfortable, find a friend or several and march your pigmented arses through those gates. You deserve to be there. You need those natural benefits more than anyone. Don't deprive yourself of them on account of what a privileged and ignorant racist may say or think!

In nature, nobody has to buy a drink, nobody has to stand in a queue, nobody will look down on you if you're unemployed and NOBODY has to be anything more than what they already are, no matter what they are. In modern society, we are constantly estimated and valued by our ability to produce output and this is because of what existing structures demand of us. All of us then, under downward pressure, identify too heavily with modern society and place huge pressures on ourselves not just to produce output but to be seen as human beings free from prejudice and vicious judgement. You can offset this, even if just a little, when you understand that the trees you walk past every day love you for the way you breathe. Birds don't demand you to turn up every morning on the dot. Foxes won't show you anger if you take a two-hour lunch. The woods don't charge you entry. Nature asks nothing of you. You can just be.

If we all come to nature, we can begin to identify with the natural system ahead of the social constructs that cause us to buy into man-made belief systems such as race and gender. And once we transcend those belief systems, we can meet each other as true equals. Nature is the perfect platform for this.

So let us take a walk and break free from these horrid chains, and claim the free health benefits that Mother Nature affords us. Let us equip ourselves with the tools, ever abundant in nature, to reclaim our sense of identity and return to modern society with a new direction to take our collective narrative in. This is not for the benefit of Europeans to better understand us; that is their task to undertake. We will reclaim our identity and aim for a greater control of our story for the benefit of future generations of people of non-European descent.

In my own experience, nature has been the constant backdrop of my development from an incredibly ignorant and uneducated boy into a more informed, well-rounded and slightly more educated young man. I had left two schools and had no sense of direction because I had been made to believe that there was no future for me beyond options so awful that I do not care to share them here. Trying to think about who I was was like trying to catch smoke, due to the fact that I was constantly pressured by school and/or my peers to produce output in particular ways; to go against my true desires. But it was years and years of weekly trips to Richmond Park that allowed me to build a firmer idea of my identity, and thus a greater sense of direction and purpose in life.

I remember vividly the first time I walked through the Richmond Gate. As I stepped into the park, it was truly as though the concrete mess behind me had disappeared and, in front of me, a massive carpet of greenery and forests began to roll out into seemingly endless space. How inspiring. I could see no bounds and was allowed to think without limitations. My mind, for once, was operating independently of my body. It had finally been liberated from working in accordance with an identity that had been handed to me from the day I was born. I could feel the gratitude my mind offered to me. It was grateful to return to its natural state and to be allowed to remember its original form which is formless, nameless and full of love. Everything we learn, particularly in modern Western life, shackles our miraculous mind until we become over-encumbered with issues. It is in the entanglement of forced circumstances that the blazing fire of our minds can become dimmed. It is behind all of the clutter of our daily lives that our mind's true power, warmth and love can be hidden. By removing ourselves from these troublesome contexts, we can remind ourselves of who we are and who we are meant to be.

I had read online that Richmond Park was full of deer, but it was the incessant noise of the ring-necked parakeets that would really strike me. I recognized their call almost immediately. The ring-necked parakeet was a species that I had had the pleasure of seeing on my childhood visits to Sri Lanka. I was fascinated by them being here, and I was also confused at the fact that nobody else was losing their minds at a literal parrot making its home in one of the busiest and greyest cities on Earth! They splashed colour all over the sky and gave me a strong sense of being at home, at a time when I felt well and truly lost. I required no plan; all I needed was to follow my heart. And, as it turns out, the population of parakeets in London does actually derive from the Indian subcontinent, which would include Sri Lanka. My ties to my motherland were guiding me through this matrix that is the modern Western world, and seeing those birds for the first time confirmed for me that I am never far from home if I look closely enough.

# THE BALANCE BETWEEN ALL LIVING THINGS

There are very few relationships more natural than the one between birds and trees. One almost guarantees the other. What's more interesting is that certain trees are more likely to attract particular birds because of the fruit they produce, the insects they attract and sometimes just because of their height. There are many reasons why birds love trees and many reasons for you to as well.

Try identifying these five tree species using the shape of the leaves, the average height and the bird species which love them as clues:

**SILVER BIRCH** – 20m (65ft) / goldfinch
**HAWTHORN** – 7m (25ft) / blackbird
**ASH** – 30m (100ft) / green woodpecker
**OAK** – 20m (65ft) / Eurasian jay
**HOLLY** – 12m (40ft) / European robin

If you live in a different part of the world, try finding five tree species that are local to you, then see if you can spot their avian visitors.

# 2

# CHALLENGING PRECONCEPTIONS

I want to start with a story. In 2021 Nadeem and I were invited by a brand to experience their product in Lake Windermere. Neither of us had been to the Lake District before so we were excited to explore this beautiful part of the country. Nadeem was delighted to leave the big city and wasn't afraid of letting everyone on the train know about it. We were put up in an incredible Danish-inspired apartment built into the trees, and we spent the next couple of days birdwatching and hiking up the many peaks.

On one of our last nights, we decided to hit up the local town (a few bars and pubs across the lake). After exiting the ferry, we walked down the hill and saw a row of bars. We picked the busiest one and walked through the door. As we entered the establishment it was like a scene from an old western: the silence that hit the room landed like a sledgehammer to the face. Lake Windermere isn't known for its diversity, but this bar was white front to back...and everyone, I mean every single person, stopped what they were doing and looked in our direction. Clearly this was not our first rodeo, so Nadeem and I picked our seats right in the middle, ordered our drinks and kicked back...

First impressions count in this country and the two ruling bodies that identify, divide and categorize British society are race and class. The reason that race has to be included is, in large part, because Great Britain – that little island with grand ambitions – colonized around a quarter of the world from the 16th century onwards. In the name of the reigning monarch, the commanders of the British Empire ventured out with their armed forces across North America, Africa, Australia, New Zealand, the Caribbean, the Middle East and Asia. They imposed laws and educational systems, and set up trade routes for sugar, spice and slaves, spreading the English language around the globe like an airborne disease and reinforcing the notion that, by possessing wealth and power, a person was made inherently superior in status – a theory-cum-structure most rigorously imposed on dark-skinned peoples across the globe.

Hundreds of years later, the ongoing result of a broken system is a Western world with distinct racial disparity, where unconscious (and conscious) racial bias is passed down from generation to generation. Due to the clever machinery of political propaganda, what might have been the unifying factor for white working-class people and people of colour became the weapon that destroyed us. White working-class people were taught by governments (and a history of cities and institutions built on wealth generated by slave labour; wealth whose true origins were never acknowledged) to fear the 'Other', coaxed into believing that it wasn't corruption and greed that prevented them from attaining prosperity, no. It was their darker-skinned neighbour, cunning and inhuman, hell-bent on stealing their money, jobs, women and dignity. As long as poor white communities were busy focusing on how to a) survive and b) terrorize their perceived enemy, governments could continue operating and strengthening a system designed to benefit the rich and oppress the poor. This perfectly oiled machine was so well produced that its power has endured to our present day and, with some light modifications, has started an additional mission on the dehumanization of refugees, migrants and trans and non-binary people.

Slavery in Britain may have 'ended' in 1833, but there is still a loud and active part of society, featuring individuals from all tax brackets, who have inherited the idea that the Black race is inferior to them. You can see it in their eyes. In their microaggressions. As Black people, we have developed the ability to sense it before it starts, in the way one might feel the atmosphere change before a downpour of rain. Racist abuse does not have to be delivered through violence or derogatory words; it can be viciously subtle. It can rear its terrorizing head in a second worried glance from a passer-by on the street, or in a shopkeeper's grip on the counter while he keeps his eyes on the domed mirror, or in the tension of a walk through a community which has few to no residents of colour. Just like Nadeem's trepidation at Richmond Park, there's hesitation and paranoia in the unfamiliar because of the experience of growing up Black in the UK. Racism is a universal experience for people of colour in the West. Every family has a sad tale to share of immigration, racist neighbours and failed integration. It is what connects us to each other beyond skin tone. Our individual stories are unique but will follow the same threads of experience with racial discrimination. As people of colour, many of us have walked a more painful path than our 'indigenous' white counterparts. We all experience the same life challenges, but in addition we people of colour have been assaulted, abused, murdered, shut out of spaces, accused of being aggressive, lazy or rude, refused entry into bars, fetishized, forced to spend hours walking home unable to hail a taxi at night, and this is just the loose topsoil of issues we face on a daily basis.

Racism is rife in our towns, cities and villages. Children learn the traits from their parents and environment, reiterate them in playgrounds, spread them to office floors and leak them onto high streets as they mature. The fight against racism is far from over. After 2020, when we saw George Floyd's murder play out on screens, the Black Lives Matter marches across the world and the contentious black squares being shared on social media platforms brought conversations about race to the forefront. The hope of change burned as brightly as it had done in various eras of the

Civil Rights movement. The world rallied behind us in a moment for the history books, presenting itself like this was going to be the tipping point for Black people's struggles across the globe. And while some things have changed in our industries and the social landscape, the systemic issues are still in play, and the institutions and individuals that uphold them remain in power and are clearly as resistant to change as they've ever been, no matter what they present outwardly.

When the subject of racism in Britain is brought up, the first seed of conversation will always grow into a tree of sprouting questions, opinions and debates. The topic is passed around panel discussions, dinner parties, classrooms and gatherings like a collection basket making the rounds in church. We listen with anxious anticipation – is this room full of friends or foes? The hope of a positive outcome largely disappeared decades ago. Accounts of our lived experiences aren't enough, and even speaking in the language of objective data and research falls on wilfully deaf ears. While there are still people in public and private forums happily debating (and legislating on) whether I am deserving of the same human rights and citizen status as white people, I know that real change still sits ahead on the horizon.

My upbringing is similar to that of many second-generation Black kids. My parents worked tirelessly to ensure I had the best start in life. Some of my earliest memories revolve around them sitting me down after school and making me practise pronouncing words. For hours we would go over the correct way to say things in the Queen's English. I hated it. At the time, I couldn't understand why they were putting so much effort in. It was only years later that I realized what was happening. They were trying to make sure that I didn't inherit their Nigerian accent. My parents didn't want me to be discriminated against because of the way I spoke. What must that feel like for a parent to have to tutor their child so they can fit into the silhouette British society wishes? The unconscious education from my parents extended further when we went shopping. When walking around Woolworths department store, my dad would tell my brother and me to keep our hands in our pockets so we wouldn't arouse suspicion. We thought my dad's rules were absurd and overprotective – a sneaky way of stopping us from fighting in the aisles as siblings do and controlling our behaviour in the store. We had no clue that these seemingly abstract rules had anything to do with our race.

My first experience with overt racism was when I was about eight years old. I had just moved from a multicultural school to a less diverse Church of England primary school in Coventry. The pupils were still quite culturally mixed, but every member of the teaching staff was white. One day I had a disagreement with a kid in my class, and he turned around to me and shouted, 'You Zulu warrior!' I was so young and naive, I didn't immediately realize this was an insult, a code word. I thought Zulu warriors were cool, but I inherently understood through his delivery that it was meant to be rude and disrespectful. Why did he think it was okay to throw out a racial slur of that magnitude and meaning? Where did he even learn this language? Was it from his parents, from the films filled with racist stereotypes they watched on TV?

Do more people think like this? How can you stop these views on race being passed on to the next generation?

I get it now. I understand the weight on my parents' shoulders in those first years of planting roots in this country. They didn't want any excuses for people to cast a bad opinion about us. Without knowing it, we were ambassadors for our people; with every shopping trip we were judged not just as a family, but as a collective community of people of colour. The view was that if we behaved in public, spoke well, dressed presentably and excelled in school, we would be one step closer to proving the racists and bigots wrong. Fuck that. Now that I'm older, if I notice I'm being followed in a shop, I will not hesitate to flip the behaviour and call out across the shop to staff or security guards, 'Is there a problem? Why are you staring at me?', immediately making the situation embarrassing for everyone present. There are so many complexities that people face when they are stereotyped. Some people can walk past prejudice, some people can't.

For many, when you are constantly labelled negatively it can lead you to question absolutely everything. You think you know yourself, but when you're told something different your whole world changes. It can leave you utterly lost. This begins at school – a place that is meant to not only protect you but also prepare you for the rest of your life. As children we're confused and easily influenced; we believe what we're told. We arrive carrying the high hopes of our parents but can quickly find ourselves outcast; at that age we have no idea about the complexities of stereotyping. We exist day to day trying to fit into a mould and internalizing every negative comment from our teachers. The lucky ones manage to make it through that foundational period, but Nadeem and I are among many who were left feeling let down; stepping out with an extra weight on our backs, a weight that moves to our shoulders and becomes a chip. And this is where the building blocks become shaky.

As you move into adolescence, and again into more white-dominated spaces (most industries), chances are you're going to have to prepare yourself to manage that 'friendly banter' of stereotyping just to survive, so it's not about preparing to go to HR but preparing yourself to still deliver under these exhausting conditions. Today there are groups that you can lean on for advice and support, but this is a recent development. For all of those who came before this period, they really had to be soldiers. There was no one to raise this issue with or, if there was, do you know how grating it is having to sit opposite someone who has zero idea or interest in understanding your experience, all the while telling you they 'get it'? And for those who aren't so lucky to have had the support to get them through, there is the possibility of taking all that abuse on board and developing an inferiority complex, which can lead to the individual taking on that 'inferior' role. It's a lose–lose situation, however you look at it, if you're a person of colour. This can have a huge impact on you until your dying day. But we are not the stereotype. We are individuals with endless possibilities in how we exist.

Just before the dawn of the millennium I made the decision many people of colour have to consider. After a decade of dreading hearing my name being called out at registration in class, I decided to go by a different name. Instead of being a victim of ridicule and the whole room bursting out laughing at the sound of my full name, Olaolu, in my late teens I took on the name Ollie. So many of us feel the need to do this to fit in. We anglicize our very existence, and the first port of call in the integration is our name. Why did teachers constantly struggle with names that originated in places further than Basingstoke? This isn't a unique experience; this is shared by countless of us. It's actually funny when we reel off the craziest of names we've had to correct. But we all know what's really going on. They can't be bothered to learn how to pronounce your name correctly because they place no value on it. What's in a name? For those of us whose names are native to our ancestors' country, they are gateways, keyholes through which we can find our histories, traditions, cultures and national pride, a grouping of letters that connects us to our homelands. Taken into Western contexts, a name can also become a source of pain, a signpost of difference, an outward reminder of Otherness. A reality that hits home when you're applying for jobs and wondering why you never even get a reply...

A 2019 study by Nuffield College Centre for Social Investigation found that British citizens from minority ethnic backgrounds have to send, on average, 60 per cent more job applications to get a positive response from employers compared to their white counterparts.[2] Researchers sent nearly 3,200 fake job applications for both manual and non-manual roles to a recruitment site between 2016 and 2017. The positions included chefs, shop assistants, accountants and software engineers. The fictitious candidates were all British citizens, or had moved to the UK by six years old, and had identical CVs, covering letters and years of experience. The only thing that the researchers changed was the applicant's name, which was based on their dreamed-up ethnic background. They found that, on average, 24 per cent of applicants of white British origin received a positive reply from employers, compared with 15 per cent of minority ethnic applicants applying with the identical CVs, covering letters and experience. Where minority ethnic applicants had to send an average of 60 per cent more applications to get a positive response from an employer compared to a white British person, the figures were much higher for applicants of Nigerian, Middle Eastern and North African origin at 80–90 per cent. The survey concluded that discrimination in the workplace against Britons from a Black or South Asian background had not changed in over 50 years.

It is a stone-cold fact that we are blatantly disadvantaged in this country because of our race. At the time when I was applying for jobs in the late 1990s, all we could do was adapt to survive. The changing of my name was a part of that evolution to an easier life in a historically white world. The start of my career is where the assimilation of my name Ollie took hold and developed a life of its own. It is where my name became more of a 'brand' than my actual identity. As more work rolled in, I was involved with larger clients and, with my agency's success, the press followed.

Could this be down to having a more easily pronounced name? I will never know, but the name Ollie just stuck. Even today, when introducing myself for the first time, I struggle with choosing to use my real name or my 'brand' name – a dilemma many have experienced when weighing up whether to take that next step in 'becoming British', since there may well be discrimination and bias at every stage of your career. Even for this book there was an internal debate over what name I should use on the cover.

I am proud of Olaolu. It is me, my culture, my heritage. Those who know will use it; it's for the inner circle. For the rest of you, c'est la vie. We live in a discriminatory world where it is easier to get through life without having to painfully respell and over-pronounce your name on the phone or be prejudiced against because of a foreign-sounding name. It is a sad fact of life that these incidents of both subtle and overt racism still happen today, so we are forced to lean into the struggle.

In my first year at university, I was living in shared accommodation with people from all over the country. A couple of months into the first term, a Welsh student said to me point blank, 'I had never met anyone Black in my life before moving in with you. I was shocked to see how normal you are.' The statement hung in the room for a long period of silence. Stunned, I didn't know what to reply. It was as if he was waiting for me to thank him for the compliment. Just another example of the ignorance we face and must laugh off in order to keep it moving. For a while we played along with the jokes and jibes because it was the easier road to take. Deep down, we were sick of it. Today, we won't stand for it.

In many environments, it still seems to be okay to be ignorant and starkly rude about racial differences. Can the casual racist be excused for dropping dumb jokes at the pub because they didn't know any better? Could their preconceptions be blamed on a lack of education about race? 'Ollie, you aren't "*black* black"', some of my white friends said to me growing up. They were trying to explain why I was *cool* and why I was different 'from the others'. What they really meant to say was, 'you're not the stereotypical Black person'. It seemed that my African heritage skipped the queue when it came down to xenophobic friendships. Did I get an automatic pass into the white crew conversations because I spoke well, dressed right and threw cool parties?

After 2020, we really hoped things would change, remembering all those Instagram posts from people saying they would stamp out racism whenever they saw it. How's all that going, by the way? It's crazy to think that before that they had the confidence to be so blunt and to come out with such shocking statements. I snapped at my friends, calling them out for their casual racism and false naivety. I stood up and told them that they were basing their view on what they had seen in the media. And when I couldn't be bothered, I'd cut them out of my life like scissors through silk. They expected me to play the role of the token Black friend, dress like The Fresh Prince, dance like Michael and rap like 2Pac.

Is it down to people of colour or society to stamp out this behaviour? There are moments of clarity that can make us snap out of our perplexity. We've all been there, that first encounter where it is clear the other individual has never interacted with a Black person before. I make sure I am open and personable from the first handshake. Initially they are cold, but then when they realize that you speak well and are friendly with an engaging personality, their face changes right in front of you. I always find it funny watching an icy stare slowly thaw into the glimmer of a smile, and witnessing warmth spread to the eyes and cheeks. This scenario and our role within it are the result of the conditioning we have to go through in society. From a young age, we are taught to be aware of and manage other people's experiences in a way that white kids don't have to. It's an obligation I resent. Being open and personable should be a common courtesy, not a matter of self-preservation.

With Flock Together we have these encounters a lot, as we venture to outdoor spaces where people of colour aren't usually found. Whenever we're out walking, it's interesting to see how we're perceived. Comments are always loaded with a level of astonishment: when people hear how passionate and excited we are about birdwatching and the great outdoors, they immediately warm to us and go from cold to super-fan in a matter of seconds. Those people with hardened preconceptions need to witness our humanity first-hand to break down the tall wall of prejudice they hide behind. As the charm sinks in, you can feel them thinking, 'Oh, Black people aren't that bad.' I achieve this dynamic by having the self-confidence to know that I am more than enough. My charm shines through and magnetizes others to match my energy. I have had no choice but to believe in myself. I know I am worthy of every engagement I attend; my presence in anything is valuable; if anyone has a problem about the colour of my skin, it is their issue, not mine. Their crass opinions will hold them back from true happiness in life; I will not be anchored by their views. If they have preconceived notions about me or my people, my work ethic and the charisma I put out have always proved them wrong.

If I take you back to my story from Lake Windermere, after a few drinks the atmosphere in the bar slowly changed. Nadeem and I were enjoying ourselves and I think it was the invitation for those around us to want to join us. Before you knew it, the majority of the bar were either sitting with us or plucking up the courage to speak to us. We ended up having quite the night with our new friends, even if we had to scold one for getting too confident and dropping the N bomb while telling a story. There will be a point for all of us where we will be given a choice of fight or flight, see-sawing between assimilating or staying authentic. It will take everything in your being to be fearless and speak out to overcome everyday racist preconceptions. You have a voice: do not ever be scared to use it when speaking from the heart. The world can be a hostile place for people of colour, filled with double standards, microaggressions and unconscious bias. As individuals and as a community we need to protect ourselves; we have to build that resilience, even if right now that means forever living in a state of paranoia, on your guard, waiting for the *when* something will happen or be said, not the *if*.

As someone who has spent their career as one of the few Black creatives in advertising, I am interested in the role the media has to play in the preconceived ideas people have about people of colour, and Black people in particular. The impact of TV on our minds and mannerisms has a lot to answer for with regard to the state of the world today, and continues to play a huge role in the evolution of race in Britain. In technicolour, the media has influenced our cultural values and the core principles in which we exist as a collective community. Before the dawn of social media, television hugely influenced the general public's views on race, gender and class. For decades, broadcasting has drawn a picture of Britain's perceived beliefs, attitudes and behaviours. The 1950s were a time when it was commonplace for white actors to blacken themselves to play African or Caribbean roles, with *The Black and White Minstrel Show* being a prime example. For twenty years, millions and millions of British homes watched the Saturday night primetime show on the BBC, whose popularity peaked at 16.5 million viewers an episode.[3] With spin-off performances in theatres and seaside resorts across the country, there was no getting away from blackface and I cannot imagine what it must have been like for Black children at school in those days.

In 1957, Cy Grant became the first Black person to feature regularly on British television, giving daily calypso renditions of the news on the BBC's *Tonight* programme. The previous year, he had starred in *A Man from the Sun*, a dramatized documentary about a group of the first Caribbean settlers arriving in London. The show cast a light on the harsh realities of the prejudices Black people encountered trying to integrate into a predominantly white community. Grant said that he 'suffered the indignity of seeing white actors blackening themselves and giving themselves bulbous lips to play black parts, reinforcing the caricature of us as black people, a caricature which casting directors, artistic directors and playwrights themselves refused to allow us to escape'.[4] A qualified barrister and actor with dozens of acclaimed roles, including *Othello* at the Phoenix theatre in Leicester, Grant suffered at the hands of typecasting throughout his career. Fed up with being overlooked, in 1973 he co-founded the Drum Arts Centre in London to showcase and launch Black artistic talent. There were limited opportunities for Black actors in the 1960s and '70s, so Grant took it upon himself to create his own market with opportunities to celebrate his culture on stage. Despite the projection the media had of Black people in the news and the open hostility towards us at the time, from pain came progress.

In 1968, Barbara Blake Hannah became the first Black female reporter on British television in a non-entertainment role. Trevor McDonald soon followed in 1973 as a daily news anchor for ITV. Their presence challenged the status quo: they led the way, opening the door for us to follow, and showed us in living colour that anything, including primetime TV, was possible. By 1976, the first ever British television series with an all-Black cast had aired. *The Fosters*, starring Lenny Henry and Norman Beaton, only survived two seasons, however, before being cancelled. Shows like *Empire Road* and *Desmond's* soon followed, further highlighting our struggle by using comedy and drama to deliver impactful stories. By the 1980s, the soap opera *EastEnders* had regular roles and storylines for Black actors, and films like *The Color Purple* and *She's Gotta Have It* celebrated and spread the joy and pain of Black culture across the globe. The evolution of race on celluloid leaped from Black people or white actors in blackface being presented as childlike, animalistic, lazy caricatures in the early 20th century to the more modern stereotypical roles found in the 1980s and '90s. We could now play the athlete, the funny sidekick or comedian, a happy 'African', a deadbeat dad, a criminal or tramp, slave or druggie, or an angry Black man or woman. For anything beyond this realm of caricaturist characters, Black people were generally not yet considered.

Slowly but surely Britain's eyes were opened to racial discrimination and prejudice in their living rooms. As the decades progressed, we as a nation were no longer colour-blind to our problems as a society. Presenters like Moira Stuart and Andi Peters not only became household names, they also became a part of our family. Seeing 'one of us' on television or the silver screen was inspiring and brought tears to our grandparents' eyes for good reason. Today, TV channels are on high alert when it comes to any racist stereotypes. And things are moving forward through varied programming; from director Steve McQueen's *Small Axe* series to the return of *The Big Breakfast* on Channel 4 with an all-Black cast. With the media's representation of race evolving towards an equality we deserve, shows like Michaela Coel's *I May Destroy You* are winning awards and inspiring a new generation of Black writers and actors. Young people now have a flourishing pack of Black role models and other people of colour to look up to and emulate. These people are not there through tokenism, which many white people would like to believe. No, these people are there because they are qualified. They are the best people for the job. When we are given the platform to create, the world benefits: go check the industries that have improved exponentially when Black people are no longer locked out. When Virgil Abloh was named artistic director of the menswear division of Louis Vuitton in 2018, he brought a different world view and a huge fan base to a historic French fashion house – and his clothes were a commercial success. There is a boom in Black publishing, with authors like Marlon James and Bernardine Evaristo winning major awards and finding large audiences. We innovate because we pull from places and perspectives that are new and fresh. The resilience we never asked for now affords us super-human creativity. We tell stories that have never been told before, and who wants to hear the same story told over and over again? Jordan Peele, the director of *Get Out*, said: 'I don't see myself casting a white dude as the lead in my movie. Not that I don't like white dudes. But I've seen that movie.'[5] It's true, we've all seen that movie before. On screen and on the page, white has long been the default setting, with stories by and about Black people were relegated to the fringes, not considered candidates for 'mainstream' success. Along with *Get Out*, there are films like *Black Panther* and *Moonlight* – films that should not have done well, from what we've been told; films of which it was said there was 'no audience'. All lies. These films blew the doors off the film industry and breathed fresh life into a space where now so many people of all colours will benefit. There's a confidence in the way we approach creativity because today we've managed to figure out all the complexities we've been dealing with, we've harnessed that ostracization into inspiration, and we're no longer letting someone else's insecurities hold us back. We have the power and strength to build our own space; no more asking for permission.

For those of you thinking 'where is the nature? I bought this book for nature', here it comes. The term 'safe space' has become popular over the last decade, in reference to a place for (often marginalized) people to come together to feel comfortable to share their experiences, away from judgement, unsolicited opinions and the need to overexplain oneself. In my experience, pretty much the opposite of a white-dominated environment. It took me a long time to realize that my safe space was outdoors, within nature. If my working environment ever gets too much for me, I will always fall back into nature to reset. In the great outdoors, the trees and birds don't judge you or take their issues out on you; the meadows don't close themselves off from you or make you question your right to be there. What I came to love about being in these open spaces is how there is no pressure on me, I'm on no one's clock or schedule but my own, and my thinking and potential can feel limitless. There's no better place to be inspired; no better place for new ideas. Nothing here matters: off-key comments hold zero weight against a clear, unobstructed

horizon. I always return to my desk renewed with a fresh energy topped up by nature's free gifts.

And these benefits are clinically proven. Walking, as with exercise across the board, lessens symptoms of depression and anxiety (which are linked to experiencing racism), while at the same time improving brain function. According to clinical psychologist Gemma Harris, this is because 'oxygen saturation and blood vessel growth occur in areas of the brain associated with rational thinking as well as social, physical and intellectual performance'.[6] I now understand why I wanted to be outside so much as a kid; it wasn't just escapism or avoidance, but because I actually benefitted from this time spent running through open fields and climbing trees.

Inspiration can strike at any time and be delivered in any form. For some it arrives through the media, culture or people. For me, inspiration came from my friendships. After playing football professionally didn't work out for me, I was certain I did not want to subscribe to a stereotypical career path. I believed we, as a Black community, contributed far more to society than just sport and music. I thought I had much more to offer and felt I could step into any sector. I had collected friends from all different areas across the country and drew influences from their varied wisdom, being open to the weird as well as the wonderful. Just like being out in nature, I welcome getting lost: losing orientation only opens the door to discovery. Nature has a beautiful way of guiding you to where you need to go. Nature, if you look hard enough, will always show you the signs. When it came down to choosing a career path, I was confident that there were no doors or industries closed to me. I was not scared of choosing something out of the box because I had these experiences with my friends who represented a huge spectrum of interests.

I decided that I wanted to take on a creative industry and be an inspiration to others in normally closed spaces. Advertising is important because it is the lens through which we see the world, so if I could ensure we were represented fairly then I would feel I was contributing. I have always had an inquisitive mind; it's the reason why I have been able to adapt so easily to any space. I am naturally interested, always happy to listen and learn, love research, and have the conviction to give you my perspective on most things, even if I sound stupid. Going into advertising was my way of challenging preconceptions and hopefully opening the door for others around me to follow. It was a calculated risk, but the hard work is paying off. Our collective effort as a community in succeeding through adversity is astounding. It is down to us to continue to innovate in every corner of the world. Especially in the natural world, not behind a computer screen or newsfeed.

My first real advertising job was at an agency called Poke and the client was the children's charity Barnardo's. The project was incredibly progressive and, for me on a personal level, it showed me the power in creativity when working with marginalized groups. At the time – having worked on smaller projects for the likes of Adidas and Nike, two brands that have mastered talking to the youth – I was able to take learnings from culture and bring new life to the tired charity sector through this project with

Barnardo's. It went on to win awards, but what I came away with was the understanding of great storytelling to land otherwise serious messages.

When we launched Flock Together, I was fifteen years into my career in advertising, where I had carved out a niche for social impact and delivered projects for many of the top global brands, helping them build and empower communities. It was a no-brainer for me to bring that expertise to Flock. On a personal level, I'd received immense benefits from birdwatching but was very aware that this activity wasn't seen as *cool*. The image was old, white and tired, but that was a preconception in itself – the Western view on an activity that has been around for centuries and practised across the world. When I met Nadeem, I could finally share my passion and, because of my career in the creative industries and his unique understanding of birdwatching, it was the perfect storm. We opened our passion to our community and, because as humans we innately seek out new things, we were able to grow immediately. The barrier to entry to birdwatching is incredibly low, so I knew we wouldn't have to work hard to get people to try it for the first time, but if you add a social element to it, which I found missing across the activity, then people will want to share their experiences. So, even if they weren't interested in birdwatching at first, I knew people would want to be part of something fresh, different and exciting.

With the mission of opening up the world of birding, I got my head down and looked at all the ways we could possibly make it more appealing, from the messaging to the documentation and the creative aspects. Everything we do at Flock Together has been considered: if it can work for global brands, then there is no reason why it couldn't work for Flock. The only difference is that Flock is a truly independent platform, with the sole purpose of benefitting our community. Brands and institutions are filled with egos, stakeholders and shareholders. Each season they have to conjure up a new agenda to keep their audience engaged and, as we all know, audiences are getting wise to these tactics. The outdoors as an industry has also been plodding along quietly for decades. With an ageing consumer base and little appeal to the younger generation, nature-bound institutions have been on high alert with regard to adding freshness. Flock Together has arrived like a blueprint for them, and this global outdoors movement we're experiencing is in part because they have finally taken notice of the marginalized groups that went ignored since forever.

There can be a tendency for our communities to feel alienated from nature, fearing that these spaces may be unwelcoming. The outdoors industry up until the latter part of the last decade had been very tired, the image of middle-aged men in khaki real (I know so, because they still dominate in a lot of the boardrooms of these brands and institutions). In the first twelve months of Flock Together, we must have had meetings with the majority of the organizations that dominate the outdoors space. There were times when Nadeem and I would be on back-to-back calls for five days a week. We felt like we had to speak to everyone because they were all so open to collaborating. What it told me was what I thought: the outdoors is desperate for new ideas. New ideas are what give longevity to companies that make backpacks or binoculars, new ideas help attract visitors to parks and nature reserves – and we had ideas for days; our ambition saw no limit.

But in spaces where we have no presence it can also be extremely frustrating. There were many organizations that were just trying to jump on the bandwagon because we were 'flavour of the month'. There were also people who came with those condescending preconceptions we've talked so heavily about. One instance stands out for me when we were on a call with a company which I won't name. This call had been in the diary for weeks, postponed and rescheduled a number of times, because the Head of Marketing (or similar title) was busy. When we finally jumped on the call, the man in question appeared on the video link in a boardroom with his blue button-down shirt and khaki trousers. He clearly had been pestered to take this call with us by his team because he didn't know too much about us. So as the call played out with a quick intro from both sides, he began to tell us, after the mention of the Flock community, that the brand regularly 'supports underprivileged groups'. As soon as he dropped this clanger I saw Nadeem squint, holding back a screwface. I proceeded to inform the gentleman that nowhere does it say that we're a disadvantaged group. Why does the word 'community' automatically equal 'brown and poor' to a lot of white people, rather than just 'a group of people with a shared interest'?

Flock Together wants to bring new thinking to the outdoors space and the natural world. Our members are made up of professionals from every sector: we have teachers, therapists, lawyers, film-makers, doctors, musicians, scientists, artists, and many, many more. In a world where white is seen as default, we are proudly present and have untold stories to tell. The response to Flock only proves further our point of innovating. We now have a regular slot on BBC primetime in the form of *The One Show*; we've worked with global brands in bringing new audiences to the benefits of nature by replacing advertising with breathing exercises across shop windows along Oxford Street in Central London; we've built stages in green spaces to give next-generation artists a platform to have their creativity seen; and we've drawn on input from our female members to design a hiking shoe to appeal to an audience that has for decades been underserved by the industry's 'shrink it and pink it' approach to designing for women. These are just a few basic examples of what happens when we step into spaces with fresh thinking.

We are not surprised when the public finds what we produce appealing and innovative. We have always known our worth. Our presence here today tells a story that transcends generations and the oceans. No matter what we've been exposed to in life, the 'banter' we've had to deal with at school or work, or the negativity experienced on the streets, we must remember that we are a part of a rolling tapestry of time. We are standing on the shoulders of our ancestors, carrying the baton and pushing for change with each step. As we rise, the community progresses forward with us.

We are unique, creative and brave, and we can be anything we want to be. Don't let anyone tell you any different.

# A BRIEF AND BASIC BIRD GUIDE
# TO AID YOU ON YOUR TRAVELS

### RED KITE

They are unmistakable in the air, with a forked tail, a large wingspan, and a bend in their wings. They ride thermal wind pockets during warmer months, soaring high in the air, but they can fly pretty low too. White patches on both their wings can help with ID!

### LONG-TAILED TIT

These cute little balls of pink fluff can often look like flying lollipops because of their crazy long tails. They are only tiny so can be easy to miss, but they travel in flocks from tree to tree so look out for movement among the leaves!

### SKYLARK

This bird is a summer special, but it's pretty easy to recognize. If you hear a bird blabbering away without rest, it's probably a skylark! It's small–medium in size and brown in various shades. It's also famous for flying directly upwards in a display to claim territory and attract mates.

## REDWING

This bird is slightly bigger than a blackbird and arrives in the UK from Scandinavia in winter. It's easily recognizable for its high-pitched chatter and the red patch under its wings!

## GREAT TIT

An easy spot for any level of birder! Present in gardens and parks, they are happy to visit bird feeders. Usually seen in pairs, or among a flock of other tits, they can be distinguished from the other tits by their bigger size and the bold black line which runs down the centre of their belly.

If the birds above aren't found in your part of the world, see if you can track down three other locals and two seasonal visitors.

# 3

# NATURE AS MY HEALER

NADEEM

The mind is the single most valuable thing to be bestowed upon any living creature. It is the medium through which the intelligence of life can be expressed. And not the 'test paper, work your life away at a bank job' kind of intelligence, either. It is the intelligence that gives any being its sense of purpose. The mind is also the home to an identity around which the intellect can revolve. For the human being, a well-tended mind can live on into ever-expansive views of the distant future. A great mind produces great ideas and prompts great actions in accordance with those ideas. The world then receives such an action and is required to facilitate it. The ideas are created by the mind, but it is the actions of the body that create impact in the *physical* world, and it is *these* actions that can go on into eternity like a wave.

Just how might a person act throughout their day if it had

started with a good deed being done to them? If they were to decide to be kinder that day to any being they came across, even if they did so under subconscious influence, this would be an example of an idea living on beyond the person who created it. Are you not more likely to smile at another person if they smile at you first? Ideas that are acted upon are ultimately what shape the world around us. It really is that simple.

I like to think of it in terms of the following: if we accept, as science tells us, that matter (anything that takes up space) cannot be created or destroyed, then an interesting idea pops up. All the stuff in the world – that's the people (including you and me), the trees, the cars, the factories, the forests, the smell of freshly cut grass, the air, the ocean, petrol, even outer space, everything! – is composed of molecules that have never ever been out of existence. This means that the parts that form you have always been here, and will continue to be here long after any of us reading this are around – even if our bodies, as we know them, flail in temporality.

We bounce around randomly in a state of constant manipulation and influence by other living beings. In this way, we are like fallen leaves being pushed, pulled and grappled by the winds. It is the *human* being, however, who has the honour of conscious 'free will' and the capability of bringing highly influential ideas to life in order to shake things up, redirect things, *create their own destiny*. Never underestimate the divine gravity of this gift. We are in control of not only our own destinies, but the destiny of all others too. We are caretakers of this planet, and each action we undertake has its own unique connection with the rest of the world. We are birthed from the Earth and gifted with intelligence, empathy and higher thinking. We are capable of sharing information with one another at prodigious rates and across great distances. These are all the necessary tools needed to take care of the Earth. We are lucky to be human beings, even if we suffer at the evil hands of a few of our own.

If you never throw a stone into the lake, you will never create any ripples. What's more is that, while you are not throwing stones, somebody else *is* throwing stones into the lake, creating their own ripples for their own reasons. Be wary not to become too dazzled or too discouraged by the ripples of others. Life is a massive lake and each of us has a pocket full of stones, each with its own purpose. The more stones you throw, the more ripples you can make. And while the ripples are as temporary as the living beings who cast them, below the surface something interesting will happen. Over time, the lake becomes filled with more and more different stones and purposes. The ripples are most visible but, underneath, the water in the lake slowly seeps through the stones in order to nourish the land with minerals. All life which relies on the land to survive will be sustained by the minerals, in the same way that we all live in accordance with percolated ideas, narratives and systems in modern society. In context, we, as people, are the ripples on the surface which fade over time, but the stones, our ideas, will last for many lifetimes and will metaphorically filter minerals throughout the land, affecting all surrounding living beings.

What we can also observe here is that matter acts in accordance with something of no matter: an idea. Now if something has no matter, then it cannot be bound by physical laws. After all, what is the limit of the imagination? It is this quality that makes an idea (and the mind that creates it) one of the most powerful things we will ever be lucky enough to experience. A single idea can become an entity in and of itself when people subscribe to it. The size of the idea, though, is dependent on how many people have subscribed – a key difference when compared to the physical object or living thing, both of which can only ever exist as units of one size and are merely the mediums through which ideas can be expressed. Even if two individuals find millions of other beings who are identical to themselves in terms of beliefs or needs, they will only ever be two individuals, whereas the idea they share becomes more of a singularity. Let's try to break this down with a real-life example.

Two brilliant football fans both support West Ham United, the best football team ever to have existed throughout the history of the sport. The two people, as *physical beings*, experience life independently of each other. No matter how much they get on as people and as football fans, they will never be anything other than two totally separate people. However, they support the same *one* football club. Their separate minds become aligned and exist in unity in some ambiguous and intangible place in time and space. So what is the football club? The players? The stadium? The badge? The owners? The toilet staff? The traffic jams on match day? It's kind of all of that and more. The football club is an *idea* that transcends physically limiting definition and can only be quantified by its influence on the physical world.

Flock Together is the perfect example of this. As an individual, I had benefitted greatly from the practice of birdwatching. I had permitted myself to slip away from the chaotic and ever-present demands of daily life in the city. I had found a place that demanded I slow down and take in all the sights, sounds and smells on offer. The slower I moved, the more I managed to see. How wonderful.

I knew that this place (nature) was healing me and I knew that, no matter when, where or how I turned up to it, it would always heal me. Over the years that followed my first ever bird outing, I would become more and more stable and secure in my life and identity, respectively. I tried to convince friends of mine that birding was the way forward but perhaps couldn't articulate myself as adequately as I can today. None of them came. I realized then that I would very likely be birding on my own for many years.

Fast forward about a decade, and I had the good fortune to have my first interaction with Ollie, when I was naming all of the birds he had posted on his Instagram. Perhaps I was trying to show off... Perhaps I was trying to test him. Ollie quickly replied and, within a few exchanges, he had presented me with the chance to become part of an idea which I truly believe has played – and will continue to play – a part in the healing and greater benefit of our community. The idea that birdwatching is 'cool', and beneficial, was with me as an individual, but it wasn't until I met Ollie that

I realized that that benefit could be opened up to a community. Ollie pitched me the idea and I was instantly sold. Even by the first walk, which a maximum of fifteen people attended, I didn't really see the bigger picture. I thought it would be a very tame group of people going out and about, enjoying the bird life to be seen in the quiet pockets of nature in the city. I didn't yet have the vision and the clarity to understand that what we were doing was a radical act and something that had the potential to change the landscape of our society for many years to come. I have only Ollie to thank for not only inviting me along for a ride he knew was in store (as he told me when we first met), but also for being super-patient with me as I bumpily tried to keep up with how fast Flock Together had started to move.

What Flock Together represents is an idea that has grown to affect communities the world over. It is an idea that can obliterate preconceptions for our generation and instil entirely new social norms for generations to come. I have learned much about the power of the *idea* from Ollie, and regard him as one of the greatest teachers I have ever been lucky enough to learn from, as he has shared his expertise in organizing not just Flock Together but many other communities. If I were just some birder, trying to get people into the woods, I would have failed; as I did with my own friendship circle. Ollie knew how to 'make it make sense', and that's all an idea needs to become great. It just so turned out, in Flock Together's case, that the 'sense' was me. I was a person who could represent a community in a familiar way but had legitimate knowledge and expertise in a field with which that same community wasn't too familiar. This is the importance of representation. While we as people of colour (a term I use warily, although I accept it's accessible, because it's so close to calling people 'coloured') face a slew of racially charged preconceptions, Flock Together – one man's idea – has removed one of them for us. Black and brown people do belong in nature.

Flock Together as a community is now represented by thousands and we hope our family only grows stronger, bringing new ideas and fresh energy to all of the outdoors, as well as the everlasting fields of tomorrow. I am happy to provide our humble group with great bird information and experiences, and will use my position acquired through Flock's innovation to create waves in nature-related spaces, which will hopefully inspire my community to follow suit. Ollie will detail what it takes to build such a community in the following chapter (see page 101).

An idea is as big as the people who follow it. Once we accept this, we can begin to appreciate not only the value of each individual mind in making an idea great, from its conception right down to its implementation, but also the value of multiple minds and the way in which their subscription sees a higher chance of survival of the idea in question. It's in this way that the community within Flock Together helps the idea to grow. You can start a business but, at some point, you must convince people to share your vision in order for the idea to increase its influence on this realm of existence. This is because, while our ideas exist in boundless space, our bodies are incredibly limited. How peculiar that something so infinite relies on something so limited to exist.

But, in the most basic terms, that's all that this life is: people, their ideas and the people who follow or fight against them. How could the world look if every human being was aligned in terms of ideas?

At an extreme degree of this notion, one idea could, in theory, shape the world for hundreds of years. Look at racism. Europeans, as individual governments (which themselves are composed of individuals), came together and constructed ideas about the world and its people. They then spread these ideas throughout the globe and, more importantly, acted in unison to enforce the will of these ideas. By dehumanizing the African, using evil media campaigns and psychotic literature, the European elite – that is, the governments backed by their scientists and lobbyists – caused the world, and in some cases Africans themselves, to accept false ideas of the African.

This pumping of ideas into people's heads creates a psychological fallout, which lives long in the memories of the people involved and of following generations. This takes shape in the real world, when people start to act on what they *believe*. And they then cause molecules to act according to these beliefs. This is bad news for people of colour. The European elite were allowed to brutally mistreat African people because a majority of the European public were duped into thinking of the African as something less than human. Less than them. But, oh, how we still suffer at the mercy of the idea called racism, thanks to its many supporters and enforcers, both human and systemic.

This, however, is a good opportunity to notice how many

things in life exist in dualities. For most ill effects, there are, more often than not, positive outcomes to counteract them. Ollie and I can serve as a prime example of this. People of non-European descent exist in the West within the context of preconceived ideas. Ollie and I as individuals had noticed this to be the case and had, also as individuals, managed to cope with this tiring fact by using nature as relief. In bringing an idea like Flock Together into the real world, we have created a space for our community to exist, which acts as a direct counter to the racially charged idea of stereotypes. All the energy, on every walk, is a manifestation of an anti-racist idea, fighting against the established systems that have oppressed us all for far too long. This is the wind in our sails, and to now have created a movement which spans the globe fills us with hope in the battle of good vs evil in the realm of ideas. May the effects of Flock Together ring off into eternity with deafening volume!

The human mind has a wondrous and endless capacity for potential, and so too does the collective human mind. So, have you been throwing your stones? If so, then well done, you! You are living life. You are happening to life; life isn't happening to you. If you haven't made a habit of throwing your stones yet, fear not! You are still alive and possess the single necessary tool to bring everything you and every other being desires into reality: your beautiful human mind. There's a multitude of reasons that prevent us from reaching for our stones. Some of these have been constructed by highly intelligent systematic design and so you should never ever feel any shame for the way you have lived your life. One of the most important reasons to acknowledge is that some people have more numerous and bigger rocks than others because they cheated in order to get ahead.

To move into the physical world, I can here share my experiences as a young person of both Jamaican and Sri Lankan heritage growing up in London and how much of an impact that had on my mental health, in particular. I should emphasize that this chapter does not hold the answers to better mental health. I am merely sharing my battles and expressing just how much nature grew to become my saving grace. Everybody's mental health journey looks different, but if my story might help a handful of readers then it wouldn't be out of place.

As a community, our attitude towards mental health discussions leaves much to be desired. This is a doubly harmful reality when we consider not only that we could benefit as individuals and as a collective from being more open about mental health, but also that good mental health is key in order for us to progress into a place in society where we are satisfied and not constantly putting up with the least terrible situation. No matter how much it is dressed up, the governance of the United Kingdom does not have people of colour anywhere in its interests except for exploitative labour. It never has and, until we make some serious changes within our own respective communities, it never will. Look at the proposed laws giving the government the right to revoke citizenship from UK residents in 2021.[7]

My experiences in life have certainly taken their psychological toll and I will here share some stories which I believe are useful in communicating to others in my community. To anybody reading this, you are not alone. We can do something to offset the ill-desired effects of this wicked place in which we find ourselves. There exists a paradise in this hell and it is called nature. And, for POC especially (but not exclusively), this paradise can help us get to grips with the obstacles and barriers that lie ahead of us, maliciously put in their place by the engineers of this hell.

I would and could never claim to be an expert in mental health but I did see a few therapists as a teenager, which, in itself, came with a race-related issue. All these therapists were white. This sounds like a trivial thing, but it plays a significant part in the relationship between the therapist and the person they are supposed to be treating. My biggest battle as a teenager was one of identity. I was trying to seek out my Blackness and I once had a white woman in my face talking about 'draw whatever you feel'. 'What if I don't feel like drawing, white woman? What then?' I should have asked her. There was a clear disconnect. Drawing is not something Black boys are typically encouraged to do. This suggestion would have felt like a foreign concept to me even if it had come from someone who looked like me, but coming from a white woman, the gap was just too big.

It can quickly be understood here how this lack of identification can breed mistrust and unwillingness to be honest within the young and/or troubled person of colour in therapy. How differently would I have reacted if I was to be part of a group like Flock Together? What if we were able to walk in the boundless greenery of nature and not be confined to the glum walls filled with white employees? What if POC were properly represented in the field of therapy – in the 2011 census, the population of London was only 44.9 per cent white British[8] – and able to help their own?

I was born to a Sri Lankan mother and Jamaican father, but in my house I was unquestionably a Sri Lankan. My Jamaican father had been absent from my life since I was five, and so the Sinhala Buddhist culture was all I knew. But even though I felt very Sri Lankan inside, I wasn't *totally* Sri Lankan. I was this other thing that nobody would teach me about; or rather nobody *could*. To know that I was Jamaican and that I had nowhere to *be* Jamaican was very distressing at my early age. It was a distress that I would carry throughout my childhood, and one that would go on to cause me a great deal of anguish in later years.

I remember when I first experienced this feeling, aged about five or six. I had a friend in school during that time called John. John was white and we used to get on okay. We would have made a good race-positive GAP Kids campaign. One day, John and I were cutting some shapes out together. We must have been talking about famous people and which ones we looked like, and I remember John telling me, 'You'd look like Eminem if you were white.' I remember thinking, 'Why does my Blackness gotta stop me from looking like Eminem, John? Why does my Blackness have to stop me from doing anything?' Of course, John didn't mean anything by it at the time, but what he did do was cause me to question my 'otherness' in relation to somebody who looked like him; somebody who could look like Eminem just because they had the same colour skin. It is at this point where I should have been able to go home to an environment where I would observe Blackness and understand that there is nothing wrong with being Black, but I had no such resource to gain assurance from. This made me feel anxious and unsure of myself, which eventually contributed to low self-esteem. See here the importance of both sides of a mixed-race child's family being equally present in their life in order to avoid identity imbalance, and just how easily great pain is done unto the young person of colour. Since John said that to me, I continued to stumble through life with frustrations with my own identity. This would continue until I reached secondary school.

I was a young Black man, seeking guidance on 'how to be Black' but feeling as though nobody in my house could teach me such a thing. A child seeks that which it doesn't have, so I was predisposed to adopting the ways and behaviours of the Black males I saw around me when I finally did reach secondary school. Many of the boys were very accustomed to the harsher realities of life, coming from some of the poorest and most violent parts of London. The vast majority of students in my first secondary school were of African-Caribbean descent and, due to a huge number of reasons, many of these people adopted ways of behaving which saw them perceived, or certainly treated by law enforcement and often their own teachers, as 'problems' to society or within the classroom. I can now understand that these people were not problems but instead symptoms of a problem that is deeply rooted in malicious colonialism and dehumanization of my people.

There were stabbings outside our school gates and teachers getting beaten up, and, on many mornings, we would walk into school through airport-style metal detectors. The environment was tough and, for a young boy without a positive male role model, the only option was to become even tougher in order to survive. Nonetheless, this school, despite its rankings in the school league tables, was full of vibrancy, energy and straight-up cultural influencers – metrics that are ignored by the lacklustre education system we have in place now. So much of the music that London is currently globally famous for began on the streets of East London and its surrounding culture, nurtured in schools like the one I attended.

Before long, however, the endless string of crime-related happenings and increased police presence in the school led to my mum's decision to remove me from it. By this point, I was thirteen years old, having just begun to establish my set of friends and a general sense of identity. To have this ripped away from me was distressing, but I had no choice. I was moving school, moving house and putting down new roots in Essex, home to the reality TV series *The Only Way is Essex*. If you're not from the UK or don't know this show, then please take the next few moments to get an idea of what it is via YouTube... Done? Yeah, so girls from my new secondary school ended up on that show. White, white, white!

Because of how white the area was, I struggled to find anybody in my new school with whom I could identify. This was doubly troublesome because I had already adjusted to a very British African-Caribbean school life. It was like my self-exploration had been cut short. All was not lost, though. I did manage to find people who reflected my image. The trouble here was that they had succumbed to their own identity issues. So, when we started to hang out together as a group, we were unknowingly perpetuating an image that our white environment had laid out for us, as we had no real examples of old to follow. We made our own way, but it was not being guided by ancient generational wisdom. It was the blind leading the blind.

In my new school, hearing things like, 'I can't be racist, my dog is black' was an everyday norm. There were even droves of white boys who were notorious for a practice called 'Paki bashing'. For those lucky enough not to know what that is, allow me to dampen your day a little bit. It involves a group of white boys driving around after dark in search of any South Asian they can find (usually a man). Once they find the unfortunate victim, they hop out of the car and proceed to beat them up quite seriously, totally unprovoked. These were the kinds of boys that dominated the school and, along with them, were the girls who would love hanging off their arms.

So, there we were perpetuating stereotypes, disregarding school and trying to navigate a hostile and actively racist environment. This concoction of bad circumstances caused me to become very unenamoured of school, and I would soon remove myself from the education system entirely. It was too much. I didn't know who I was, and there I was being asked what I wanted to be. What if I just wanted to figure it out in my own time? What if I didn't want to do anything except recover from the trauma of coming from an abusive and broken home? Why was there no lesson for that? It was when these questions bore no answers from the schooling system that I recognized that school was not for me. The environment I needed was one that could welcome me with open arms and demand nothing in exchange. I needed a hug, and nobody in school or my home could provide me with one.

In my youthful naivety, I thought that there was something wrong with me. Why don't I fit in? Why is there no place for me? I thought that my life and its terrible circumstances had ruined me to the point where I could not fit within society. As far as I was concerned, I had no future and the world couldn't have cared less. With my age and experience now, I realize that, if there is no place for you in this world, then it is your right to create one for yourself, and it is this message that I will emphasize to any youth who feels as though they do not fit in. There are many others like you, and you all deserve to find your place in this world. Do not give up hope because that is what these cruel engineers want. They want those who start with troubled backgrounds to give up early and remain in their unfavourable circumstances, generation after generation. BE THE CHANGE AND BREAK THE CYCLE! They don't say 'beat the system' for no reason. And remember, young ones, that you face nothing alone. We, your elders, are working hard to build communities that will always welcome you and offer you guidance and love if you ever get knocked down.

So, at the ripe old age of fifteen, I had made the decision to leave school and begin to explore *myself*. This is something I certainly wouldn't encourage kids to do. Go to school, kids. Education is important, blah, blah, blah. Having said that, something I do highlight very strongly to the kids whom I have had the pleasure of working with is that before you figure out *what* it is that you want to do with your life, you must first establish *who* it is that you are. I know the youth football teams I have coached in recent years have done many exercises listening to this kind of spiel. You do not find out who you are in the classroom. In the classroom, you are only instructed on what to do, and those instructions are designed to serve the needs of society, which is the medium through which capitalism and the status quo can exist. That isn't to say that some of the things learned in the classroom have no value; just that, under the current curriculum, there is very little to no room for mental wellbeing lessons, let alone for people of colour. Imagine if there were lessons that had your fulfilment or personal development at heart.

In schools, at the moment, the best place to find out who you are is the playground. There you are free to speak to whomever you want, about whatever; people are free to speak to you and you can gain a sense of self based on your own decisions and their respective outcomes. I believe that schools ought to have more activities in the curriculum that see different year groups learning together. The whole 'year 1, year 2, year 3' thing is cool, but what if there were some lessons that saw different year groups having to learn and work together? Why all the division and categorizing?

Having decided that I was done with school, the question to myself was, how do I ensure that I'm exposed to playground-like environments and not classroom simulations? Where does there exist a space which sees no figure of authority overseeing my every action and ensuring that my entire being is focused on serving an agenda that doesn't serve me? Again, *nature was the answer*! And while I didn't really appreciate this in my conscious mind at the time, I believe that, in my subconscious, informed by innate navigation passed on to me by my ancestors, I knew that this was the truth. It was difficult to find a place that would allow me to be unapologetically *me*, but I kept faith.

While all my friends were in school, I would often be stuck at home. Near to where I lived, there was a green space called Claybury Park. We often referred to it as a 'forest' because that's pretty much what it was. After my friends had finished school, we would go there to ride dirt bikes, start campfires, and generally do whatever the fuck we wanted. Another example of nature accepting living beings in all their states, destructive as they may be. Hanging out in a forest was a concept totally foreign to me, having lived my entire life in an inner-city environment. I really was not accustomed to a culture, in England, that had such a generous space for nature, but in Essex I learned to become comfortable in it.

I noticed that the Essex boys, while being far from perfect, did have this native knowledge of the land. It was in Essex where I would experience my first campfire. A bunch of white boys and a few of my friends would regularly meet up in the evenings, deep in Claybury Forest, and have a party around a campfire. This was mind-blowingly fun to me at the time. These boys knew how to start a fire and, not only that, they knew the best (most secluded and safest) place to do it, and they acquired this knowledge from older boys who had done the same before them, older brothers who had long left the school. Over time, a reputation was built of this area as the ideal campfire spot. See here how the idea of the first little shit to start a fire there lives on through kids who have no idea who the originator was, and how this is achieved through generational storytelling within a community.

What I took from these fireside escapades was that, even though we had all gone to school together and had run around being little shits together, these guys had a world of knowledge, about which my posse and I had little clue. This intrigued me at the time and motivated me to seek out green spaces more actively. I would never have gotten this inspiration were I not exposed to the moment that triggered it. Observe how the relationship between organism and environment is such a beautiful and delicate balance that the two begin to resemble each other over time, like the common potoo (*Nyctibius griseus*) and its camouflage... Google is your friend. Not only this, but how easily the course of an individual, particularly a young person, can be changed by what they are surrounded by. Thank you, Mum, for doing your best to place me in a beneficial environment.

Having adopted a small part of this rural subculture, there was a day where, by chance, I decided to sit in a graveyard, which was connected to a smaller, local park not too far from Claybury Forest. All my friends were in school, and I was committed to giving myself the time to explore myself and assess my life as a whole – something which is incredibly difficult at the best of times, let alone when under the pressures of teenage angst and racial identity issues. This sounds pretty morbid at first. And while I do think I was suffering from depression and PTSD (post-traumatic stress disorder) at the time, it is my whole-hearted belief that, if left unprovoked and allowed to exist in a state of complete freedom from attachment to people, places or things, the mind, particularly that of a young person, is liable to find solutions to problems.

We all have a subconscious mind and, when we accept this, what we acknowledge is that there is a part of the whole self which is controlled by something separate from the conscious self. This other subconscious part, then, could therefore only be controlled by a completely separate source or by a part of yourself with which you are wholly unfamiliar. Whichever one may prevail, it would certainly be a good idea to become familiar with the part in question. To sit, in silence, and to perform no action except the act of breathing, is the only way, apart from sleep, to become familiar with this mysterious governor of your mind and, indeed, your body. This, in effect, is meditation.

Meditation as a concept was not so foreign to me, having been raised by a Sri Lankan Buddhist family. Buddhism teaches that being a Buddhist is simply an approach to life. Now, in my upbringing, I didn't ever leave the temple feeling as though my life had changed. However, I did manage to change my life by making decisions based on the temple's teachings. Self-awareness is a massive part of Buddhism, as is the understanding of suffering as a part of life. The suffering, though, exists as part of a harmonious *balance* (touched on in Chapter 1) between suffering and joy, the idea being that neither one should be allowed to influence your decision-making. This is an incredibly difficult habit to pick up because, as we have established throughout this book, human beings acquire their sense of self, as individuals, by interacting with the world around them over the course of their life. We enjoy being of use to our loved ones, as well as the feeling of being loved, just as much as we despise an unpleasant person or a person doing us wrong. The natural inclination of the living being is to familiarize itself with things that are pleasant or helpful to it and to avoid things that do not tickle its fancy. Buddhism is almost the opposite of this. A human being should aim not to seek out or avoid anything, but instead to be open to all possibilities of life and allow all moments, 'good' or 'bad', to pass by undisturbed and uninterrupted. Observe here the parallel between one of the benefits of nature and a fundamental principle of Buddhism: allowing positive and negative moments and memories to pass freely.

Love is love *always*; not just when it's convenient or when there is something to be gained. With this wider context, it is easier to understand why I sought out a graveyard to try to get a grasp of what was going on in the world around me, as well as inside my own head. The graveyard, similar to the forest, was incredibly quiet and contained no relics of capitalism. There wasn't anything immediately visible to remind me that I had to 'become' something, as if what I already was wasn't sufficient. In fact, what *was* visible to me were lots of gravestones. Relics of death. Oooooooh scary!

Of course, this is a very depressing thing to imagine at first. A young boy, out of school, hanging out in a graveyard – simply tragic. And while tragic things were happening, and had happened, to me by that time, the glaring presence of death ultimately had a positive effect on my pattern of thinking. The backdrop of numerous graves evoked thoughts of reflection in me. It caused me to appreciate the fact that I was alive. A markedly different thought to a fear of dying. I do not fear death, for I believe that there is no such thing. Bodies may expire but souls, influence and *ideas* live on forever. (With this being said, the fact that I am here, alive, today, as a human being of sound enough mind to write down these ideas and experiences and share them with the world, is a fact I cherish greatly and do not take lightly.)

By exposing myself to an environment like a graveyard, I allowed myself to face, not only my own wide-open reality, but also an ever-present possibility for every living human being. The way in which we exist in today's society disconnects us from this possibility. By removing ourselves from the idea of our own death, we take away our own humanity. We take a step towards becoming less like a living being and more like a machine; an object designed to serve a particular function until our parts become old and wear out, at which point we are replaced by another machine. This should not be the fate of any human being; we should be able to explore ourselves every day until we figure out, *for ourselves*, along our *own* journeys, who it is that we are and what it is we would like to do with our limited time. Are we as human beings not worthy of this freedom? The fact that exploring ourselves and chasing our dreams is most often a 'risk' is massively problematic. I am not saying that you should seek things that bring you near to death, but rather that you should seek to do anything in order to love while you are alive and allow only love to provide your direction. That is love for yourself, the things you do and those you share the world with. Do not let 'security' deter you from doing so. THAT is what being alive is all about; following your heart, passions and interests freely. Don't you ever let a horribly corrupt system rob you of that simple birthright!

To be surrounded by the memorial stones of people who did not have the privilege of being alive really did fill me with motivation at the time. It was almost as if the souls of the people were whispering words of encouragement through the gentle winds. I saw in those gravestones full lives, lives cut short, hopes, dreams, husbands, wives – *people*! They were no longer able to enact their will as human beings; how lucky am I then to have my free will perfectly intact? It was as I reflected, staring out at the entirety of the graveyard, that my attention was finally broken. It was broken by a bird that I had never seen before, and it was striking for many reasons. Firstly, it was a bright green bird!

Having grown up in London, I had only become immediately familiar with a few species. While I admire all of these (crows, pigeons and seagulls) for their adaptability and intelligence, they are usually rather muted in their colour compared to the bird that was presenting itself to me. Not only was it bright green but it also had a marvellous red cap, which contrasted perfectly against what I can only describe as its black 'mask'. I was really in awe of the crafting skill that Mother Nature was showing off. While I had never seen this bird before, and had no idea which species it was, I did recognize one thing: it had a really long, pointy and sturdy-looking beak. This could only mean one thing: a woodpecker.

The woodpecker was sifting through the grass around the gravestones, dipping in and out of view as it weaved between them. It was clearly looking for its favourite food, which I know now to be ants! I grew to learn that it is fittingly called a green woodpecker (*Picus viridis*). (Seriously, though, google 'green woodpecker tongue' – they're adapted to eating a shitload of ants.) I wanted to capture the moment, and so ran home to grab my camera (Canon, holler at me). I came back to the same spot and, sure enough, the woodpecker returned. It didn't stop there. Through my more focused observation, I soon saw kestrels, long-tailed tits (*Aegithalos caudatus*), nuthatches (*Sitta europaea*), and many more. I didn't choose the bird life; the bird life chose me.

As I watched these creatures go about their business, something struck me. I became quite fixated on the duality of that particular moment. There I was, removed from two schools, no plan for a third, still a year left of school to go, struggling with identity and feeling like absolutely nobody cared and, yet, here stood this creature of true beauty, going about its daily life without the slightest bit of knowledge of my endeavours. How profound, gracious and wise this creature was without any effort. I learned that, even though my life is tough, it will go on. This may sound wishy-washy, but there is some substance to it.

Capitalism moves on from a struggling individual in such a way that the individual in question falls behind in the 'race'. All your colleagues could be progressing at work while you take the day off because you can't get out of bed. Everybody is getting up and going to the party while you stand 'still' at home. What becomes evident is that, unless you have a specific capitalistic function, you are not allowed to join the party. This breeds alienation, seclusion, and further onsetting of depression and worthlessness. Everybody is too busy building upwards to stop and see if you're okay. They busy themselves because they fear being in your position. How horrible a dynamic for all involved. The difference between capitalism and that green woodpecker is that the green woodpecker didn't exclude me. It made me feel welcome. One of the most beautiful creatures to walk (or fly) the British Isles had offered me the blessing of witnessing it, and it asked nothing in return but basic respect for not only itself but its environment. My sex, gender, race, physical ability or religion played no part in that woodpecker's decision to land six feet from me and go about its business. Nature at this moment was reminding me that I deserved the best from life at a time when I had almost forgotten such a truth.

It can be hard to react in new ways, particularly if the situations you find yourself in are reminiscent of a situation that previously caused you trauma. Trauma inflicted at an early age makes life difficult to navigate, particularly if you have no guidance. In my case, at five years old, I witnessed horrific violence in my home and the effects of this stay with me until this day. I was riddled with self-esteem issues, issues of identity as well as masculinity. This experience with the woodpecker gave me what I felt was a perfect counter to such terrible feelings. The woodpecker and its grace afforded me the chance to see that I do deserve the beautiful things that the world has to offer. This instantly boosted my self-esteem. With sufficient self-esteem, an individual is more likely to healthily express their needs and wants, and will be better poised to make decisions – and, more importantly, *better* decisions – because they believe themselves to be deserving of positive and beneficial outcomes.

There have been many phases in my life where I have fallen into lulls of depression. I have travelled to Central London alone for nights of drinking that have seen me face-down in my own vomit on a closed train platform (shout out to the police officers who picked me up and put me in a black cab that day). I have been in bed for days on end, fearing to leave my room because I had no job, no prospects for work, and I was ashamed to face the people with whom I was living. Depression can feel like you exist as this terribly insignificant part of a wider network, which would be happy to see you removed from it. There is nothing to be seen beyond, 'Anything I try, I will fail at because I am unworthy and incompetent'. Once this type of thinking sets in, even going to the bathroom can prove to be a tiresome ordeal. Your mind pins you to the spot, discouraging you from gaining perspective from the wider context of the world.

That's again why this woodpecker was such a game changer. The chance to see the ethereal woodpecker again, or rather the chance to go and see the endless number of beautiful creations of nature out there, was a powerful motivator to get me out of my bed. I was compelled to travel to new places like Richmond Park, the White Cliffs of Dover, the New Forest, and many more beautiful spaces, in the name of birding. Along the way, I would see new places and meet new people, and soon realize that there *was* a world beyond my bedroom and it *did* want me as a part of it. What's also important to note is that I was providing these wondrous experiences *for myself*. This filled me with confidence once I started to reap the benefits of nature.

Nature makes me feel good; when I feel good, I make better decisions; better decisions make me feel good; and it goes on and on. I had forged a way to a happier state of mind as well as a promising future, using only Mother Nature and the British railway system (at least it's good for something). *This* is the power of nature in all its accepting, loving and beautiful glory. She will not yield to the will of capital, she will not discriminate in the name of agendas, she cares not who serves her, for she has boundless love to give! Mother Nature graciously gifts us a life, which we all hopelessly cling on to so dearly. We run around trying to 'make the best' of our lives without realizing that life itself is the best thing about life. But, of course, this is hard to appreciate at the best of times.

For a moment, in the closing of this chapter, I would like to inspect a regular human interaction. What do you say if somebody gives you something? 'Thank you.' Those two words of basic gratitude rest at the cornerstone of what makes us human. They are symbols of our appreciation for any new thing we may receive. My question here is, where is our thanks to nature? How do we symbolize our gratitude if we are so grateful for this life we have been given? Say thank you to nature by exposing yourself to it, learning about it, valuing it and protecting it from evil! She has given us so much and, at the hands of a few soulless individuals in our human community, she suffers. These people must be removed from their influential positions and replaced by *minds* who have love and nature at the forefront of all priorities because, no matter what you believe, we all come from nature and we all need love. Nature has shown us that she is always on hand should we need her, but now that she is under threat, can we offer her the same service?

# A BREATHING EXERCISE

Find a quiet place under the shelter of a tree. Focus for a few moments on nothing other than your breath. Breathe in, through the nose, for eight seconds. Hold the breath for eight more seconds, then exhale until the lungs are completely empty. The aim is to be still in body and mind. As the body does, so the mind will follow. To help achieve this, you can focus your eyes on the tip of your nose.

Aim to sit under the tree, focused on your breath, in silence, for at least five minutes, and afterwards write down five thoughts that passed through your mind, whatever they are. You can go into as much or as little detail as you wish to. In these notes, you will begin to see the things that float most heavily through your mind. When these things are identified, the reason for them being significant to you can then be examined. Next, write down a reason, or several, that you think caused these thoughts to circle around your head.

It is through this continued practice – in the quiet and in tree shade – that a firmer grasp on identity can be established. Identify with nature, identify where it's missing in your life and, once you've found it, protect it with all you've got!

# 4

# BUILDING A COMMUNITY

OLLIE

It takes a village to raise a child. As we grow up, every interaction and experience we encounter goes towards building the foundation of our personality and character. Our environment and the surrounding community become the threads that help weave our identity. From day dot, the world we live in is incredibly small. We learn about life from parents, relationships through relatives, friendships with classmates, and mentorship from teachers. Collectively they become our extended community as we hurtle towards adulthood. Influence on a young person's life can also come from outside the community. Television, film and music open the mind to new interests that may lead to lifelong passions and new pools of people to meet. The internet, especially social media, plays a huge part in connecting and disconnecting modern-day civilization as we know it. But our home life, social circles and academic achievements ultimately affect our future decisions and behaviour within society.

A community creates a culture; it is the blueprint of a united journey. As we get older, we naturally have questions about how and why the world works the way it does. This is especially the case if you're a child of colour in the West. If your questions about class and race cannot be answered by close contacts or social circles, and there is no one to connect with in the wider community, what do you do? Influence from the right community can inspire the next generation to aim higher, work smarter and truly believe there are endless possibilities to what can be accomplished.

Impactful lessons can be learned from shared experiences, or from the passing of knowledge down the family tree. In the last chapter (see page 72), Nadeem talked about the impact and influence of shared ideas: some have the power to change the world for the better, but some have the potential to cause harm. The wrong influences can lead to disaster and result in life-changing choices with no return or undo button. The relationships made in your formative years become the base ingredient for your prospects as an adult. The stronger the support system, and the wider and more diverse the community, the better chance a child has of living a rounded, fulfilling and happy life. But what would happen if a child had no community to turn to? Would a lifetime of feeling like an outsider have a lasting effect on their outlook on life and future achievements?

I will always remember those slow steps towards the front of church, knowing that all eyes were watching us from behind. Wide eyes and whispers signalled our arrival, the Olanipekuns, the only Black family in an all-white church. We were a proud Nigerian family that had moved from Bristol to Hillfields in 1987, when I was three years old. It was just my mother, father, older brother and me in an otherwise multicultural community in the centre of Coventry. Even though we were now in a pretty rough area, my parents felt lucky because we lived in a terraced council flat near a church. Together as a tight unit from the beginning, we had no cousins, uncles or relatives to turn to in England, a new country for my parents, which we called home.

Along with all the Nigerian flair and passion for worshipping my father was hoping to impart on the stiff church folk, my parents (like many other African parents) understood that religion would help aid a warm integration into their new chapter of life in the United Kingdom. At that time, my parents had only one route to survival in the country, and that was to assimilate through Christianity. They had no choice; back then there was no manual they could follow. There are many more resources available to people in their situation today, online or through support groups.

My parents were committed to keeping our West African Christian traditions alive, symbolized in their traditional dress – wax cloth that was always pristine, in every colour of the rainbow but never clashing. For me at that age, each robe was a new target for simple minds to ridicule. It was our misfortune that the local church had not progressed like the cosmopolitan Coventry, the city famous for birthing the 1970s music group The Specials and the anti-racism movement 2 Tone. From the very first time I sat down on the pew I did not feel comfortable in my surroundings. The churchgoers were as grey as the weather, and the sermons felt like they would never end. I was made to feel like an outsider with every hanging gaze and side-eyed stare. These microaggressions are confusing for a young child. The congregation found the African sermons my father held comical. He put all his energy into every reading and psalm, but his efforts fell flat in attempting to share his heritage with a community that had not been disturbed for generations.

It was at a time in England when white working-class people were made to believe these new Black faces were there to take their jobs. This hangover carried well into the back end of the 1980s. If you were of Black origin walking alone, there were police officers, the National Front and even old ladies who saw you as a target. As an African child growing up in Britain, you would be hyper-aware of these ops on a daily basis. Ignoring second glances from muted mothers, or racist remarks said 'in jest' outside pubs, became second nature to us. We were made aware of our differences in both the most brazen and the most subtle of ways. Sometimes, a single look while walking along the high street would make it clear you were not welcome.

As I grew older, my attention in church waned further. During the summer months I grew taller, stronger and more vocal. From then on, I started to be singled out and scolded by the deacons.

They were unable to relate to my experience and, as a result, I couldn't engage. They didn't understand me and had no interest in trying. They were conditioned to believe I needed extra discipline. This lack of imagination and concern is a reality for most Black people across Britain and, in my case, it led to early experiences of discrimination. Nearing my early teens, it was only a matter of time before I'd be confronted with wagging fingers on a Sunday morning, inevitably followed by my full name, Olaolu Olanipekun, being shouted over outdated hymns, with every vowel pronounced spitefully wrong.

My parents worked hard day and night. My mum, Joy, was a nurse with the National Health Service for fourteen years before becoming a lecturer in health and social care. My father, Isaac, started out as an engineer and went on to be a lecturer in maths and physics for the Royal Air Force for over twenty years. Back then, my parents had high hopes for their children to become successful and to pass the baton of health and heritage on to the next generation to prosper further. Even with big dreams and high accolades, along with the many hours spent serving the country in healthcare, education and national security, as Black people my parents were never heartfully accepted. They were knocking on closed doors, unrelenting and committed – not in order to break the doors down, but to have them opened, accompanied by a respectful, dignified invitation to come inside. By buying into the great British dream and planting roots in middle England, they wanted to pave the way for future generations of families.

To keep me off the rough streets of Hillfields, my parents signed me up to the Cub Scouts, who promised to deliver a 'safe' space every Saturday. I couldn't relate to any of it. I struggled with the practices, the regimented formality, the language that was used, the uniform we wore, but mainly the absence of any role model willing to understand my Black perspective. Someone in that position of trust should be able to see beyond their own lived experience. The Cub Scouts had football, so there were no complaints from me at first. However, even with the chance to run around a field in a competitive game I had wanted to play for years, I still did not feel comfortable around these people. The organizers were disciplinarians, shouting, blowing whistles and speaking down to us at any given opportunity. And as the only Black kid in my group, I was singled out. If you are young and Black you can't connect with that. The Cub Scouts as an organization was not set up for the Black experience, but neither had it grown with the population to be considerate of this. Their behaviour alienated me and, with no established relationship with the organizers, I could not engage with the activities. They were not my people. I lasted about a year before getting kicked out.

In recent years, the dark past of Cub Scouts founder Lord Baden-Powell has been exposed. In 1896 he was responsible for the deaths of Zulu rebels in southern Africa, and in a 1939 diary entry he called Adolf Hitler's *Mein Kampf* 'a wonderful book'.[9] When it came out in the newspapers, the Scouts PR machine went into overdrive, signalling systemic racism in society and admitting that their organization was not 'immune'.[10] They created a reading list for leaders that included *Diversify* by June Sarpong and *Black and British: A Forgotten History* by David Olusoga. They also asked all staff to be anti-racist. Too little, too late, too vague. But it does help explain why I experienced racism first-hand from staff on camping trips. This attitude came from the top and trickled through the organization.

What the Cub Scouts did do was introduce me to the outdoors. I admit, I wasn't ecstatic about the camping trips and excursions. At ten years old the idea of a whole afternoon of knot-tying in the rain was not my idea of fun, but it beat being in a church or classroom. Looking back, being a Cub Scout gave me a better understanding of the outdoors. Every Saturday I was reintroduced to open space. I didn't realize it at the time but, when left to my own devices, I felt at peace in the open air; the outdoors had a grounding effect on me. Camping may have been a gruelling activity, but doing it made me comfortable with setting up a tent, keeping fires alight and sleeping under the stars.

Later in life, I would try to arrange nature walks or outdoor activities but was always surprised and confused at hearing my Black friends saying, 'Nah, that's a white thing.' It took me a while to understand where this thought process came from. The Black community in the UK tends not to join outdoor groups. We have been urbanized to believe that concrete jungles are our natural habitat, and that trips to the countryside are not a part of Black British culture. Most of us do not have the luxury of a leafy suburban park or woodland retreat in walking distance from our home. We do not have the opportunities to go climbing, hiking or foraging growing up, let alone leave our towns and cities to camp in the woods. And even if we did live near greenery and attempted those activities, would we be accepted into those circles? Again, that paranoia follows you everywhere.

Even though the Cub Scouts' mission was 'conquering the outdoors', that is not what I took from the experience. It took me many years to realize that I had the skills to find peace in nature within me: I knew how to find freedom in a field and how to claim the open space as my own. As we at Flock Together continue to unpack the issue of introducing Black communities to nature, I am learning how much work there is still to do to change the constructed narrative of the outdoors in the UK.

My first experience of the benefits of a welcoming community was on a different football pitch. After months of begging, I was finally allowed to start playing on Sundays at the age of twelve. Alongside my older brother, my teammates became the solid support network I had needed from an early age. Through the connections I made at football, I found emotional support and a new extended family. The games showed me the importance of being part of a team and being there for one another. This support we had for each other built a bond that went beyond the field. I even enjoyed the guidance from our coaches, when normally I would dismiss opinions of adults in authority based on previous experiences. I remember one coach parroting the phrase, 'If your mate's in the shit, you better help him out.' That has stuck with me to this very day. Team sports saved me, giving me the grounding I needed and the support system I had no idea I was so desperate for.

But, most importantly, the game showed me the value of friendship and what can be achieved when one is surrounded by supportive individuals with a common goal. Coming back from being outside I was always a lot calmer. As an adult, the one constant remedy I resort to when things get hard is to head outdoors. There's a freedom in this space that allows me to think with total clarity. Here, as the body is put to work, the mind can wander, and we can think rationally without distraction. Without football leading me to the outdoors I don't know where I'd be today.

What went from being a weekend hobby became an obsession. Watching *Match of the Day* religiously, witnessing the era of Cantona, Ince and Barnes hooked me in as a fan forever. But when I started *playing* football, I felt as though I was embraced by a city. With my attention at school further wavering, my success on the field gave me the accolades that I had sought elsewhere and never received. By fourteen I was kicking balls in the back of the net from the edge of the box, while being called every name you could imagine by the opposing team. The irony was that the verbal abuse and racial slurs from the parents were worse than those from the players on the pitch. This experience really toughened me up and helped me develop a thick skin, but it also made me wary of white people. I was the only Black player on my team and when it got heated no one ever came to my aid. My only option was to ignore the chanting, brush it off and hope to score another goal. Somehow, they would get away with it because I had no family support on the sidelines. My parents were busy working long necessary hours by this point, and work commitments had to take priority. I understood, but I do still wonder what that period of my life did to my psyche in the long term.

Racism has a complex impact on children. The doomsday feeling of being racially abused in your youth sticks. Life is different, the world becomes a little bit darker, you are now suspicious of new people, looking for their hidden reactions towards race. I had no choice but to bottle up these emotions from an early age, ignoring my inner turmoil because there was no option other than moving forward. It is only later in life, unpacking these memories, that one can consider how damaging it was to bury those painful experiences. As a young person searching for my own identity, being subjected to racism made me question my role in British society. At this time, I had no Black community to turn to in my time of crisis. Today's concept of being proudly Black and British had not yet been created and celebrated; we were still subjected to heavy institutional racism in suburbia.

Early trips back home to Nigeria didn't deliver what I unknowingly needed them to. In those young years, encountering the idea of decolonizing my mind was beyond my understanding. The trips would consist of being driven from one family member's house to another, day in, day out. With each new introduction to yet another auntie came the hugs and jubilation, but as a child you didn't really understand it all. Among the chaos of Nigeria it did sometimes feel like a chore rather than a holiday. Only when I travelled back without my parents did I understand and see what the West didn't want us to know about the overwhelmingly empowering nature of being in Africa, and its incredibly rich vastness of land, culture and wildlife. Nothing can compare, and I will struggle to put into words what it feels like to truly be welcomed as an adult. I remember the first trip as a real holiday and getting off the plane, feeling that heat as you step through the cabin door. Making your way through the airport, taking in the atmosphere, the sounds and the energy of the people. Even though I was clearly dressed as someone here for a holiday, I remember being knocked off my feet by a very simple statement. It came from a stranger just after the exit of the airport. This gentleman came up to me, shook my hand and said with a big smile, 'Welcome home, brother.' I don't know why this had such a profound impact on me, but it has stayed with me many years later and is still crystal clear in my memory.

Back in the UK, at school I struggled to focus on certain lessons, often daydreaming or doodling the day away with zero attention on the teacher at the front of the class. When I was mischievous with my friends, I always remember being labelled the ringleader when I knew I wasn't. I excelled in subjects I enjoyed, like history, English and art, but found certain other subjects extremely difficult and oftentimes found myself lost in deep thought in classes and easily distracted when playground games leaked into the classroom. With the relatable African parents pushing me to become a doctor or lawyer, I dreaded parents' evenings because I knew I wasn't top of my class. As an adult, I always had an inkling that something didn't feel right during my school days, and at the start of 2020 I was diagnosed with ADHD (Attention Deficit Hyperactivity Disorder). It is strange to find this out now as an adult. There was no such thing as ADHD when I was at school, it just didn't exist back then, so I was left with so much confusion and hanging questions. Am I a bad kid? Am I stupid? Discovering this has helped me bury some very uncomfortable memories from school. How I like to describe it to friends now (I'm still working out how to manage my ADHD) is that getting diagnosed has given me an inner peace. There has always been an anger present when I look back at my school experience, but now the memories are softer. I've spent a lot of my career challenging the education system, bringing to life initiatives that focus on alternative learning, because I'm a firm believer that education shouldn't be confined to the four walls of a classroom, and I'm committed to helping others like me in those crucial early years. I have no doubt there are many more young people and especially Black boys who have lived the same scenario as me and my ADHD but have stayed undiagnosed. Who is there for the countless Black schoolchildren who slip through the net?

There is a structural inequality within education for Black children. After the Education Act 1944 used the term 'educationally subnormal' to define children with limited intellectual ability, many teachers decided to deem Black children as intellectually inferior and to voice fears that too many Black pupils in a class would slow the learning of white pupils. Following a protest by white parents in West London, in June 1965, the Department of Education and Science released 'The Education of Immigrants' report, which suggested a limit of 30 per cent of immigrants in any school.[11] As a result, many local authorities took the policy as law and sent immigrant children to schools outside their local area, in an attempt to limit the number of ethnic minorities in certain schools. There have been attempts to segregate us from the moment the strategic immigration of citizens from Commonwealth countries began in 1948, with five hundred Jamaicans crossing the Atlantic on the *Windrush*. By the 1960s and '70s, hundreds of Black children in Britain had been sent to schools for pupils who were deemed to have low intelligence. Learning difficulties were mistaken for learning disabilities, and Black children were simply written off and sent to ESN (Educationally Subnormal) schools, crippling a generation's confidence. Following years of pressure and campaigning, the 1981 Education Act abolished 'educationally subnormal' as a defining category. The 1985 Swann Report, a government enquiry into the education of children from ethnic minority groups, found that the low academic performances of immigrant children could be attributed to racial prejudice among white teachers and in everyday society.[12] This news could not have filtered down into schools across the country, as my brother and I were held back and put into 'special classes' made up of every Black and Asian in the primary school. At my school, the teachers had inherited these old racist practices and branded us as unteachable. These classes were an experiment, a modern-day way of controlling who received education. Every lesson made us feel inferior.

The reported underdiagnosis of ADHD in Black children is a result of institutional racism and flawed behavioural assumptions embedded within school policies. The lack of diagnosis and treatment leads to the over-punishment of Black children; it also contributes to the over-representation of Black children as troublemakers with no prospects other than prison, otherwise known as the 'school-to-prison pipeline'. My reputation at school grew for being a rising footballer and class clown. I played up to it, but never to the extreme of when one teacher scolded me, turning to one student and spitting, 'Don't be like Olaolu and solve problems with your fists.' It was clear that a strong handful of the faculty had unfounded preconceptions about behavioural problems within the Black youth community. Their mindset was based on racial prejudices established from decades of believing white Europeans were the more intelligent race and deserved better treatment. Any protests of innocence to my parents were ignored. They believed the teachers: hearing the bad news backed up their suspicions about my behaviour and poor grades. Even when I tried my hardest to fall in line, I was still cast as the naughty kid. With no one to turn to for support, no community to console me, in juvenile retaliation I took on the role. I started to live up to the bad reputation that had been thrown upon me. At one point the atmosphere between myself and a teacher accusing me of horseplay in the hall was so heated, he ended up pushing me down hard to the ground, to the shock of everyone in sight. It was heavy: I remember being so confused as to how that could happen. My friends and I sat in silence on the bus home; the shock was very real.

Decades later, I would learn that my old school was facing an independent review investigating why so many Black children were being expelled. They declared the Church of England school was institutionally racist. Instead of feeling vindicated, I couldn't help but again think of how many Black children over the decades had been affected by a broken and unbalanced educational system. If we were just one small school in the Midlands, how many more schools across the country could be accused of the same systemic racism?

At sixteen, I travelled to New York with my brother for football trials. I had six weeks to play a game I loved, with teams that could change my destiny. The only downside mid-trip was GCSE exam results day. The plan was for my father to travel to the school to collect my grades and call me. It was a phone call I was dreading, after thoroughly struggling with revision for my exams. Reading pages from my textbooks over and over again and nothing sinking in, I just braced myself for the response even before sitting the exams. I ended up with a cluster of mid-range grades and, to say the least, I did not do well in my parents' eyes. When I returned to England, I was dragged back to school to try to retake the year, but, thankfully, the teachers refused to give me a place.

Upon my return from my trip and turning down offers in America, I enrolled at Henley College in Coventry. Along with securing just enough results to get me in, the school's focus was mostly on competitive football and less about studies, which worked perfectly for me. Even though I had begun to pursue a career in sport, my parents were disappointed because of my poor grades and lack of willingness to explore education further. They did not understand that I was being drawn into a community that truly appreciated me. Football had become my solace and sanctuary. Playing sports helped me to build a reputation based on character, not colour. I was regarded for the man I was playing with my teammates, for my endeavours on the field, not the 'problem child' picture painted by my teachers. My community was a part of the recovery process I needed. It gave me a warrant not only to exist in this country, but to thrive. Before, I was made to feel that I couldn't be Black and British, whereas on the pitch I was at home, I was celebrated by my teammates and my coaches. I discovered first-hand how the nature of birth and circumstance could shape your life. A few sliding-door moments helped me find my feet and break free of the system, but I had to be brave in the decisions I made.

Some of what my parents said finally did land and, after finishing my two years at college, I decided to go to Coventry University to study a new course called 'Communications, Culture and Media'. This was a key moment in my life where I actually considered a career, something that I was going to commit to. The course was the beginning of the rest of my life and, looking back, it really was a defining moment. More than anything, the course taught me critical thinking of the arts and validated my love for culture, which I will touch upon later in this chapter. Uni was going well, I was engaged, but as always my distracted mind had other ideas. I was two years into my course when I decided to drop out of university. I had broken through as a semi-professional footballer for Nuneaton Borough FC and by nineteen was paid £250 a week for Hucknall Town FC – not a huge amount, but being paid to play football was life-changing at that stage of my life.

While I loved having a regular income, I was forced to realize the importance of independence and being able to support myself financially and emotionally. With big ambitions always driving me, instead of blowing all my football wages on things wannabe footballers blew their money on, I pooled my earnings together with a grant from The Prince's Trust and set up a clothes shop in the centre of town, based on my love for culture. I had an idea of bringing together like-minded individuals into a welcoming space, where anyone was welcome to express themselves and escape life. Named TrampsInPrada, within three years the shop became a youth hub, a home for the creatives in Coventry.

The shop's city centre location gave me the perfect position to really understand subcultures. City centres have a way of attracting outsiders; they are places where you'll always find the widest mix of people, some looking for an escape but most looking for a like-minded community. There was a rich history of culture in Coventry that was slowly being forgotten and so many creatives were looking for a new outlet. There was a severe lack of nightclubs catering to the 18–25 age group, especially considering the musical history of the city that had birthed the first legal 24-hour nightclub back in 1990. Based on the growing community out of the store, I started organizing regular late-night events. From the shop and club nights evolved a monthly market for the arts and crafts communities; it was in these places that I learned how to build safe havens and platforms for the creative community to support, protect and celebrate each other.

It was an interesting time for me to throw myself into these initiatives, where I could test and learn without the fear of failure. Maybe it was ignorance, maybe it was arrogance, but looking back it was immensely important. A few months later, I was asked by some friends in London to contribute to a recently launched website that documented youth culture, called BNTL (Better Never Than Late). On the site I talked about all types of brands, music, travel and parties, but then saw trend forecasting, a subject I was passionate about at uni, as a great way to build my name and reputation in London. I had now found home in the communities I discovered and drew confidence from the conversations I was starting to have within these inspirational groups. What this experience taught me is that when you can't find your community, then you have the power to create one. Whether that's a walking group, dance class, art collective, supper club. Anything. Follow your gut to find your calling and then try to discover others with the same interest or common goals. There is power in numbers, strength in sound and soul.

As previously mentioned, before Flock Together, I would go on long walks in the woods to reconnect to nature and birdwatch. This was my way of resetting my system. For me, the open air and space have always been healing and have helped to settle my mind whenever I'm stressed. The creation of Flock Together was a cosmic coincidence that could not be ignored, but the ingredients are out there for everyone. Charlie Dark needs a mention here with his amazing work around the running club Run Dem Crew. I was fortunate to be around for its inception and saw the benefits Charlie brought to so many people's lives. Charlie changed running for everyone involved, opened it up, brought innovation and made it sexy. At Flock our aim was to give people of colour a supportive safe space: this will never change but, on top of that, we want to empower everyone to see the potential in collective thinking. Building your own support groups to cushion the blows of bigotry will become the building blocks to your success. Chosen wisely, the ecosystem you create will deliver all the support and guidance you'll ever need within it.

Today, institutions have let people down. We live in a fractured society, where we need all the support we can get. Family doesn't have to be a blood relative; deep friendships can be made between the most unlikely characters over the simplest of coincidences. With open eyes you will see opportunities to thrive everywhere. You just need to get out into the open air and gain that perspective. Our aim is to build a society where if I win, you win. When I eat, we all eat. The older generation closed the door behind them because they thought there wasn't enough space for others; our generation kicked the doors off the hinges; the next generation will answer to no one. There are two million Black Britons living in the United Kingdom today, all with similar but unique experiences living in this country. We belong here. Sharing our stories and learning through each other's experiences will be the language for bringing true change. Instead of whitewashing

the past, we must remember the struggle and celebrate our future. There has been a generational shift – we no longer accept the things we cannot change. We are changing the things we cannot accept. And the more we come together, the more our confidence will grow.

Throughout my adolescence I sought out communities because I saw the power in collaboration. I wanted to be challenged and was keen to learn from those with different perspectives from my own. With friends I was very fortunate to be able to create amazing platforms and see ideas come to life. The red thread through it all was the element of service: maybe my Christian upbringing did give me something, or my fight for understanding through school gave me a formula to follow. While recognizing my privilege, I saw how collective strength could provide support for the under-supported. I understood how influence could be used to give voice to those left behind in society. And I understand creativity will create solutions. In my time navigating the world of social impact, I've often found myself thinking about how confusing and intimidating all of this can be. There's so much pressure to be educated on endless social causes and to prove dedication by performing activism online for followers. Everyone wants to be perceived as 'a good person', often at the risk of expending more energy on looking like they care than on actually caring. We're all so scared to get it wrong, to be effectively cancelled if we make a mistake. This is the biggest threat to progression. Instead, I would like us all to be confident in our approach and to not fear making a mistake. It's in the effort and the 'doing' that we really learn what's needed.

Over the past few years, we've seen the constant rise of the collective; we know there's strength in numbers. A solid community will give you everything you need. But with all these collectives working in silo and thinking their cause is the most pressing, we end up missing the big picture again. An intersectional approach is the only way we will all succeed, and to get there we need to open up that dialogue. Be clear that my issue is your issue, and vice versa. A quote from an Aboriginal activist sums it up perfectly: 'If you have come here to help me you are wasting your time, but if you have come because your liberation is bound up with mine, then let us work together.'[13] In doing so, we will create a community that is defined by collaborative leadership, working together to achieve collective progression.

Flock Together began with a chance encounter over the love for nature and birds. Our community is built from that moment of connection. We have been drawn into the collective because of our common interests. It is no coincidence that we have all walked different paths to lead us to this same point. We each know that 'we are not alone'. Many others have trudged this long road before us and we too have been beaten down by the system, but together we have risen back up stronger than ever. We can change the world if you follow us. Guided by birds beyond the trees, we will help lead the way to a better future.

# MOVEMENT TO EXPAND THE MIND

If you move the body and provide the senses with new sights, smells, sounds, tastes and feels, then you are also giving your mind new references to pull from when it comes time to produce thoughts and ideas!

Move the body to move the mind. For this activity, aim to reach ten different green spaces in your local area, over the course of ten weeks. Write down what the area was called and, if you really want to do some scientific work, record the bird species that you saw there as well. What was the vibe like?

Travel safely!

# 5

# WHO RUNS NATURE?

NADEEM

Take yourself to a tropical place, a place full of life. Everywhere you look presents you with fruit-bearing trees, bountiful fish, native spices, a diverse range of wildlife, and wise people with inherited knowledge of all the above. The culture of the people in question is often integrated deeply with the natural world. Take, for example, the huge majority of residents (certainly residents I have visited) in Sri Lanka, the birthplace of my mother. My memories of Sri Lanka are warm and filled with family, although I am greatly aware that Sri Lanka's society is far from perfect. Whatever the case may be, the food is always fresh, the weather is normally great for beach lounging or jungle treks, and there is a guarantee of seeing a shitload of geckos all over the walls after dark.

Being on an island on the equator makes a good place for mosquitoes to let themselves be known, especially considering the number of rice paddies present throughout the land. Mosquitoes breed very quickly if they have access to still bodies of freshwater; as a result, mosquito nets – which are preferred to toxic insecticides – are a household staple in Sri Lanka and other countries where the insects (as well as the diseases they carry) are prevalent. Although the mosquitoes pose a huge potential threat of malaria and dengue fever, not to mention general annoyance, they are understood to be living beings fulfilling their purpose, on which human will should not try to impose itself. Buddhism teaches that imposition is ego-driven. We can see here that the Sri Lankans, among many other global cultures, have allowed a degree of understanding, and even physical space, for the natural world and its phenomena.

This understanding, and subsequent tolerance, is exemplified further by the fact that almost every building in Sri Lanka is inhabited by geckos – most commonly, the Asian house gecko (*Hemidactylus frenatus*), a species that actually shows a preference for living with humans. House geckos will be seen crawling along walls as soon as night falls, and a single household could easily host dozens of the reptiles. Why is there, then, no gecko extermination business in Sri Lanka? Surely somebody is missing a trick there! Well, no, they're not. The geckos spend all night tirelessly hunting insects and the like, from mosquitoes and cockroaches to praying mantises and spiders. The people of Sri Lanka created an industry to produce a non-intrusive solution (mosquito nets) to a problem posed by nature and, in turn, nature has expressed its truly intelligent design, by solving the perceived problem of the human being. By permitting the initial 'pest' to exist freely (while still taking precautionary measures), the people of Sri Lanka, by inaction, have allowed for nature to find its way of restoring order and balance, as well as gaining service from an animal species which, as it turns out, thrives in human-filled environments.

This level of understanding is not just decided one day by a marketing campaign. It isn't subtly fed to people through the drip of daily media. This is age-old knowledge passed on for many a generation until it becomes a social normality beneficial for both the human and the animals involved. While it could be argued that the nets were a necessity due to the inefficiency of the geckos' work, it cannot be said that the geckos aren't helping. And it is this appreciation and value of life that we could learn from in the Western world. This effect certainly can go on to benefit the wider ecosystem. Maybe mosquitoes get the short straw, but, considering the potential diseases they carry and the rate at which they breed, that's fair enough. The ecosystem nets a benefit.

Sri Lankans differ from Westerners in many ways. In particular, the way the everyday Sri Lankan regards their native animals results in the small tropical island generally having a much closer connection to the ecosystem and, in turn, a lifestyle more conducive to a pleasant disposition, general contentedness and understanding for other life forms. In the majority-Buddhist country, it is believed that each living being carries a soul. Once a being dies, its soul will then move on to occupy the body of a new being (or body) in need of a soul. At the most basic level, this is what we call reincarnation. However, through good deeds and by using its human time wisely, a being can see its soul leave the cycle of being reborn.

Enlightenment (the end goal for most Buddhists) comes from practising good deeds and heightening self-awareness through meditation. This means that if a soul is to be reborn as a human being, it should make use of this fortunate situation and practise meditation and perform deeds of goodwill, as well as have a great love and respect for all life. This generates good karma for the human being. If the good karma builds to a sufficient level, it can allow the soul to transcend the physical world and begin a new journey in new dimensions. (String theory, in the world of physics, posits that our universe exists within ten dimensions, by the way.[14])

Buddhism and many other Eastern philosophies' teachings highlight the importance of all life being connected by *life force*. An individual should be able to see themselves in every other living being. How hopelessly distant we find ourselves from this sort of philosophy in the busy Western world. This ought to worry us. Our lack of connection to life (that is, other living things) only makes us more accepting of the ill doings of those who govern the way we live, when they exploit and dispose of our fellow human beings in the name of their soulless and rigged game.

Another great example of the potential human–animal relationship is the one found in certain tribes in the southeast of Africa. In Mozambique, there exists one such tribe called the Yao. The Yao have free rein in Niassa National Reserve, which is roughly the size of Denmark and managed by the Mozambique government (that's right: a single national park – within only the

sixteenth biggest country in Africa – that is the size of Denmark).
Anyway, the Yao people, in their true wilderness, have managed
to remember what being a human being is all about. They
happen to share the land with a species of bird called the greater
honeyguide (*Indicator indicator*), and their relationship with
the birds is truly amazing. The Yao have managed to figure out a
way to work together with the birds to raid bees' nests, in order
to get sweet honey. What's more impressive is that the tribe also
manages to fairly reliably summon the birds. According to a 2016
report, the tribe had a summoning success rate of 66.7 per cent.[15]
When successfully summoned, the bird, with humans, found
a hive 75.3 per cent of the time. This mutualistic relationship
benefits the humans, who obviously get the spoils of honeycomb
and honey, but the birds also benefit from the relationship.
Almost every single time, the Yao people will leave behind the
bee larvae and the beeswax, which are both highly calorific, for
their helpers. The Yao people have found a path which benefits
both them and the natural world around them, in a similar way
to the Sri Lankans and their geckos. Maybe this is bad news for
the bees, but the biggest threats to bees in that part of the world
are forest fires. While fire is used as a method for calming the
bees, more forest fires are started through farming, and so 'hive
hunting', as it were, isn't the real threat in this respect. The felling
of the host trees also promotes diversity in the canopy, giving a
chance for smaller, less established trees to grow. The ecosystem
ultimately nets a benefit. The practice is overall sustainable, as the
data in the study would suggest.

This knowledge of the land and its inhabitants is passed down from generation to generation, and creates a collective culture of true integration with nature, to the point where there is no distinction between the two. In the Western world, we have the opposite. Mostly townspeople (in 2019, 82.9 per cent of England's population lived in urban areas), we are torn from nature and thus from our own true identity.[16] We are then given new ideals and priorities for our intellect to gain motivation from, but even then these ideals will influence us to no longer spend time with our fellow human beings or to carry mistrust for them. It is this conflict of interest that the conscious human being, in the clutches of Western capitalism, battles with on a daily basis.

This battle continues until a glorious (but difficult) path is forged, or until the human being succumbs to the will of capitalism, having almost certainly lived a life full of regrets in the name of *priorities*. In the case of the latter, we forge new identities as servants to agendas that do not meet our needs or fulfil our desires. The Yao people face no such issue, and happily continue their practices. Some scientists believe that the relationship between humans and honeyguides goes back millions of years. The birds may therefore have an *innate genetic desire* to guide humans to honey. See here an example of *true desire* being fulfilled, which ultimately has net positive results for human, animal and environment.

Let's think of this in terms of Western life. In the UK, for sure, there are tons of red foxes (*Vulpes vulpes*) roaming the streets. While they are still legally regarded as wild animals, and not as vermin, they rummage through our bins and create an awful mess on the streets. As far as most of us are concerned, they may as well be vermin. If this is the case, then we can see here the disconnect between human understanding and the way of nature. Human beings, in their bumptiousness, see it as their god-given right to leave massive sacks of wasted food on the streets every single day, but then have the audacity to villainize the animal that makes a use for it.

If someone else were to be able to control the narrative of the red fox – take me, for example – they might be tempted to say that the vermin are the human beings who create an egregiously excessive amount of waste every day. The foxes, rats and roaches we share our space with make a meal out of our rubbish, providing a very valuable ecological service, and they ought to be championed for it. What we in the West are taught is to resent nature, which is only in fact responding to a problem that we humans have created. We see here again how Mother Nature is too good for us worshippers of capitalism. Because of our excessive consumption of endless products, litter pollution still poses massive threats to the condition of our planet.

How much food do we need to eat? Or buy? Think of restaurant bins and just how much food waste we produce in our own boroughs, let alone cities or countries. Not once have I seen a consumer advert urging people to buy less food. No, that would be counter-capitalist. Instead, we live in a culture in which we spend millions of pounds on food and then more millions on waste being collected every single day from our streets. The real waste is the amount of food we consume as a whole society. It is gluttonous, unsustainable and, let's have it right, the cause of many health issues in the Western world.

When we consider the earlier examples of people from these warm climates, we can readily accept that they have a huge understanding of and, in some cases, great respect for nature, often to the point where the human culture itself is shaped by it. So, why is it then that when these people live in colder parts of the world – take Europe, for example – the stereotype is that they do not belong in nature or cannot acquire any understanding of its ways? Why do they still have no say or representation in the fields that concern themselves with natural affairs? What are the people in charge hiding in their rural affairs?

Once we have established that both human beings and the wildlife around them can exist in harmony (certainly more so than they do in the West), we must explore, in detail, an example of mistreatment of wildlife in the West and how it could benefit from taking a page out of the Sri Lankan or Yao book. We can begin easily with two examples from the UK, which will help us to explore the disastrous effects of human activity on the ecosystem and society, the failings to address these effects (and why these failings are allowed to prevail) and, finally, alternative ways in which the apparent issues can be tackled. We can also, importantly, explore how the methods of management of these issues have a direct impact on the quality of life for the everyday person, and just how closely tied to colonial practices these methods are.

Let's begin with the story of the grey squirrel (*Sciurus carolinensis*) and examine how a legitimate ecological issue is used to mask questionable actions within the British government. For those unfamiliar with *Sciuris carolinensis*, it is the squirrel that will eat from your hand in the park and, in the UK, it is likely the only species you've ever seen. They are also rife in North America, and pretty quickly adapt to life in the urban landscape. The decisions made by the UK government, particularly regarding the environment and ecosystem, have resulted in effects that have had disastrous echoes for decades, eliminating species along the way. The effect of the grey squirrel on the red squirrel (*Sciurus vulgaris*), Britain's truly native squirrel, is a perfect example of this.

How many red squirrels have you ever seen in the UK? None? Unsurprising when you realize that they have been wiped out to near extinction by the introduction of the grey squirrel. Red squirrels in Britain, in just over a century, have had their numbers drop from millions to an estimated 140,000.[17] This makes them an endangered species in England. 'Ahh, whatever man, it's just a squirrel!' Okay, cool. You can keep thinking that, but first look at how this animal and its effect on the ecosystem have been used as devices that spread inequality among people.

Grey squirrels were introduced from North America to Britain in the late 1800s by white Victorians. Harmless as they seemed to be, there turned out to be pros and cons to their introduction. One thing soon became apparent: they were breeding very quickly! It was long thought that the grey squirrels introduced to Britain travelled far distances from where they were born and so would breed quickly with other grey populations. This caused scientists to believe that there was a new 'super breed' of squirrels on the rise, with more varied and more resilient genes. There were even bounties put on the greys. Launched in 1953, a scheme offered a reward of one shilling for every squirrel killed, which soon increased to two shillings in 1956.[18] For context, a gallon of petrol back then was just over four shillings. Registered shooting club members could also claim two shotgun shells if they didn't want the money. Needless to say, the scheme was ineffective and the squirrel bounty was abandoned in 1958.

The *actual* spread of the grey squirrel is most likely down to human (English) intervention yet again, and not to some hyper-nomadic grey squirrels forming a 'super breed'. In 2016, Dr Lisa Signorile, during her PhD studies at Imperial College London and the Zoological Society of London, analysed the genetic profiles of close to 1,500 grey squirrels from the UK and Italy. The data showed that different populations were still very genetically distinct, meaning that the spread of the grey squirrel in the UK can't have been a result of them travelling great distances; at least, not on their own.[19] In fact, there were strong signs of inbreeding, which means that the squirrels stayed put wherever they'd been placed – by humans!

As it turns out, it is one of Britain's aristocrats who is probably most responsible for the pandemic of grey squirrels in London. Surprise, surprise. The 11th Duke of Bedford, Herbrand Russell, was known to gift many squirrels bred on his property at Woburn Abbey in Bedfordshire, and even released populations into Regent's Park. We can here observe the elite and their tendency to create a scapegoat (the 'super breed' of grey squirrel) to take the blame, as opposed to addressing their own wrongdoings and general incompetency. It becomes worse when we observe how the truth is hidden from public view and the reality manipulated to profit the elite until today. Notice also the massive difference between Herbrand Russell and the Yao people, with the former having extracted wildlife from one place and dished it out as some kind of commodity in another, and the latter living in harmony with the animal world and forging a mutual relationship over thousands (maybe millions) of years.

The British government's approach over recent years towards tackling the squirrel problem (because it is still ongoing) further perpetuates their lack of regard for our ecosystem and planet, as well as their willingness to line the pockets of those who reflect their historically privileged image. In 2014, the UK government launched a scheme that saw landowners paid £100 for every hectare they owned, every year, for five years, in the hopes that they could trap and/or kill grey squirrels. A similar scheme still exists today.[20] This means that millions of pounds of public money is given to landowners in exchange for culling grey squirrels. Who will benefit most from this scheme? Certainly not the red squirrels.

Take Conservative (right-wing) MP Richard Benyon, for example. He owns the Englefield estate (which he inherited), in rural West Berkshire and Hampshire. The estate boasts an area of 14,000 acres (Central Park in New York City is 843 acres), according to its website, which equates to over 5,665 hectares.[21]

From 2010 to 2013, Benyon was Under Secretary of State at the Department for Environment, Food and Rural Affairs. How convenient. If Dick claimed anywhere near what he could for squirrel control, he was looking at over half a million pounds of public funds coming the way of his family trust every year, for five years, thanks to this scheme. Even if he didn't, the point still stands that only one demographic of highly privileged people would benefit financially from this strategy.

Not only do the shameful acts of this country's government continue to reward the historically favoured, but, in addition, those with the biggest say in wildlife conservation tend often to be practically indistinguishable from those who caused the problems. Landowners are consulted before most groups on rural issues. In England, half of the land is owned by less than 1 per cent of the population![22] How unhelpful and disastrous this dynamic is for the future of our wilderness. There is an urgent need for other communities (that's us!) to have substantial involvement in the decision-making regarding issues in the rural parts of this country. It is time to put a stop to the suffering to all life at the hands of a greedy and loveless government. It is time that the ecosystem benefits from communities that want to put it first.[23]

It should also be noted that the 2014 squirrel bounty scheme was launched one year before British taxpayers finished paying off a multi-million-pound debt, accrued in 1833.[24] Why were we paying back all that money for nearly two hundred years, you ask? The answer is almost bone-chilling. We were paying back the money that was originally given – in compensation, post-abolition – to the families who had acquired their wealth by brutally enslaving Africans. Yeah, just go back and read that again. Taxpaying British citizens, including those of African descent, until 2015, in effect compensated white British slave owners. WE PAID THEM OUR OWN REPARATIONS! What kind of tyranny do we live under? Our government and law decreed that only one party involved in the abolition of slavery was worthy of compensation for the losses incurred. This happened to be the party that benefitted wholly from the foul practice and would only have lost their stolen money. The other party – the one that was relinquished to subhuman levels of society (to put it nicely) – were supposed to be happy with their so-called freedom, which, in reality, was just no longer being brutally enslaved but rather subtly enslaved. They were given no such monetary reparations, and their descendants have not received compensation either. Today, we still find ourselves subjected to the will and attitudes of the dominant party. What a warm, loving and caring environment we live in. How lucky we are to walk the streets freely, scrapping for low-income jobs, being taxed so we can literally pay our captors and, finally, most importantly, be subjected to daily racism! To add further salt to the wound, it has recently come to light just how many of Britain's landowners profited from slavery and colonialism, and used their ill-gotten gains to buy up swathes of our countryside.[25]

When we look back at the story of the grey squirrel and the methods used to solve its issues, we can see the ecosystem has been sacrificed for capital gain, and knowingly so. There is no genuine effort being made by those in charge to tackle the issue.

Rather, they will use the issue to validate their corrupt harbouring of wealth. It's just powerful white men with their greed, fucking up the world and thinking that the same greed can solve the very problems they and their ilk have caused. The willingness to rush recklessly into action without consideration for ecological impact, the generous use of violence to solve problems, the failure to engage other communities in finding solutions and the cowardly tendency to create scapegoats are methods used by the British elite to this day, and are a big part of the reason we find ourselves in an environmental crisis. The Yao people of Mozambique have not been documented, on a single occasion, trying to capture the honeyguides to make finding honey more 'convenient', as would certainly be the case in the West, where convenience rules all. Instead, the Yao have learned that if they want the honeyguide to appear, it is best if it does so of its own accord, and therefore both birds and people have learned unique calls. This is what mutualism looks like.

Flock Together has taught me that representation is incredibly important. I must here credit the genius-level of vision from Ollie, who recognized that by posting pictures of our community in nature, strapped with binoculars, we would create a trending sensation. The pictures went viral because of their 'absurdity'. An absurdity that is rooted in preconceived ideas about people of non-European descent. Why was it such a big deal to the world that some Black people picked up binoculars and decided to walk in the woods? The answer is quite sad, actually. It is because people of colour have historically gravitated to urban areas, where there is more employment and stronger communities, meaning that white people have historically – and maybe unknowingly – claimed the countryside for themselves. This means that children of non-European descent, in the Western world, particularly those living in unfavourable conditions, will have a far smaller chance of seeing themselves represented in anything to do with the outdoors in mainstream media. This causes these children to passively disengage from the outdoors and thus decrease their chances of being marketed or catered to by brands, legislation and wider society in general.

Imagine how it feels to know that you are a part of a culture which people around you take so much from, and yet they only want the bits that suit them, without acknowledging that these are a representation of a whole people with stories and substance. This is the position of the person of colour in the Western world and, strange to say, it has parallels to the condition of the grey squirrel at the time of its origin in the UK...being kept as pets, being given as gifts and having their effect on their new environment overlooked.

If we take our MP from earlier, Dick Benyon, here is an example of a little-known action by a powerful white family in the countryside quite possibly negatively impacting an urban community. The Benyan family trust literally removed about 2 million tonnes of sand and gravel from an enclosure on their estate, which was home to irreplaceable ancient woodland.[26] This woodland would be permanently lost after the work was done. The plans were approved, despite the advice from local councils and wildlife groups warning against it. This is the guy in charge of *rural* affairs at the time (2012). What a state of affairs rural England is in. Wildlife populations have gone to shit. Anyway, why would anybody remove 2 million tonnes of sand and gravel from their land? To sell it, of course. The Benyon family trust sold it to a company that supplies heavy building materials to the construction industry.[27] Again, an example of the hopelessly greedy rushing of capitalism benefitting the most historically favoured. The people of the lower classes are shut out from any involvement in this situation and they will probably suffer the most immediate consequences when awful gentrifying 'new-build' apartment blocks are erected by some building company. This displaces mostly urban communities, of which a big portion of people of colour in this country find themselves. This sets them back economically and solidifies the advantaged position of someone like Benyon. How shameful.

I think the lesson to be learned here is that if we do not change our attitude towards nature and the environment, as well as the respective decision makers, we are liable to have history repeat itself and put other species like the red squirrel at risk, which, as we have established, puts people at risk of being exploited by crooked schemes and policies. It may already be too late to solve the grey squirrel problem. But it is certainly not too late to have new, enthusiastic and fresh faces begin to write the history of the UK's rural spaces. The Flock Together Academy aims to be the space to facilitate and nurture young, curious and energetic minds, who may or may not have an interest in a career in the wildlife sector, and to show them that this thing called nature is the most prized thing on our planet. We aim to take kids from underprivileged backgrounds, regardless of their ethnic origin, and show them just how valuable a resource nature is in protecting the planet from evil, but also in helping them cope with the endless pressures that surround them in their daily lives. The hope is that, in the decades to come, there will be a new generation of radical thinkers who will prevent ecological issues from being used as a means to line the pockets of corrupt governments.

To move to our second example of ecological mismanagement in the UK, we must prepare ourselves to question social norms and how our decisions, in accordance with these norms, can have an ecological impact that contributes to the mistreatment of our dear planet, sometimes without us knowing. It is very important for me to emphasize that the work to be done to save our planet from the insidious agenda of capitalism trickles all the way down from the top to the everyday person, like you and me. This is not to say that the burden of responsibility falls on us. The brunt of the work and onus rest on the shoulders of those who manufacture the conditions in which we all live. It cannot be ignored, however, that there exists an issue in society today which is having a disastrous effect on wildlife the world over. The main contributors to this issue, certainly within the UK, do not appear to be those of non-European descent and we can explore the significance of this later. The issue we will explore here is cats. That's right, the domestic cat. The cute fluff-balls that charm their way to our hearts through viral videos, movies and other forms of pop culture. These animals appeal to our incessant need to be loved and ultimately acknowledged, which is a perfectly reasonable and natural need for the human being. We are, of course, social creatures. However, I want to make it clear from the beginning that cats pose a massive threat to ecosystems and are already implicated in significant impacts on other animal populations. To identify the contributing factors to this problem, we, unfortunately, have to look at our own behaviour and the reasons for it. To all the cat people out there: be brave, bear with me and let's get through this.

Cats are constantly used as an emotional buffer by human beings, and this overly sentimental image of them makes them increasingly desirable pets. Notice the need to *own* the animal as a means to serve a need for the human being. Cats are also an alternative to a dog, which serves a similar emotional purpose, but cats require far less effort and money to maintain. This lower level of responsibility does, though, have a cost. This cost is incurred in our back gardens, our streets and, surprisingly, our oceans. In 2008, it was reported that 2.5 million tonnes of fish were utilized directly by the cat food industry, which will no doubt have increased with the demand for cats as pets.[28]

This point becomes of further interest when we acknowledge that the population of cats in the UK is sharply increasing, mostly in cities. This is because cat population density in the UK is being influenced by human activity and not by natural prey density, meaning that 'more houses' is likely to mean 'more cats'.[29] The density of the urban cat population has led to a boom in cat numbers over a short space of time. There are now over 10.8 million pet cats in the UK.[30] When we consider that many of the cats are allowed to roam free and explore the wider ecosystem, we can see how there has also been an increase in feral populations, which account for approximately 1.5 million *more* cats in the country. The stray population is also increasing because people cannot care for the litters that their pet cats produce. This means that rescue shelters are full to the brim and simply cannot look after them all. Limited resources in shelters mean that thousands of cats are euthanized every year, contributing to the 204,000 animals euthanized in UK shelters in 2021.[31] A sad fate for any animal, particularly those that are only present as a by-product of human activity. They have not chosen this fate for themselves and yet suffer the most. A narrative that shouldn't be unfamiliar to readers of this book.

It should be noted here that cats aren't as domesticated as we think. We have been using them for less than half the amount of time as we have dogs, and the fact that we allow them so much time outside will only further prolong their full domestication. Most scientists agree that domestication of cats began around 12,000 years ago, while the same process with dogs began 30,000 years ago.[32] We are, in effect, at a major crossroads in terms of the storyline of the cat. Is it responsible to keep going in the direction we are headed? Many of the animals' perfectly natural instincts are still pretty active in their daily lives – conditioning their claws on your sofa, like lions against trees, being a good example. None of these traits show themselves more than their desire to hunt. How many times has your cat brought in a dead animal or, more specifically, a dead bird? The numbers are really and truly mind-blowing. In the UK alone, cats account for the deaths of 100 million animals every single year, 27 million of which are birds.[33] That's about 74,000 birds every single day and just over 3,000 every bludclart hour.

The objective fact is that cats, particularly those in the city, are bad news for local wildlife and have a terrible impact on biodiversity. On a global scale, cats have been responsible for a great number of species extinctions: 63 species of birds, reptiles and mammals have been driven to extinction, at least in part, by the 'domesticated' cat.[34] In Australia, cats were introduced to the ecosystem by Europeans (surprise, surprise) and, in turn, they proceeded to decimate bird populations. The cat is thought to be implicated in at least 25 mammal extinctions in Australia and to pose a threat to a further 124 species.[35] In fact, every single year in Australia, cats kill the same number of animals (about 1.4 billion) as those that died in the widely publicized bushfires in 2019–20.[36] A lot of cats were introduced to foreign lands in the name of the European crusade. A true ecological disaster in many countries, but nobody is talking about it.

I will make it clear here that I do not dislike cats, nor cat owners; I actually have great admiration for any animal which shows resistance to human conditioning. Full respect to a creature that, even after thousands of years, has not been fully domesticated, still exhibits wild behaviours and has all the benefits of a typical pet but is verily capable of hunting its own food. Boss shit. I therefore appreciate that this critique will rub (or stroke) some people up the wrong way, and I thank any cat owners for bearing with me. I am simply saying that there is an ecological disaster happening out there and people are acting like it isn't. Is it such a bad thing to question the pros and cons of 'owning' an animal that famously cannot ever truly be owned?

There are many charitable organizations concerned with the welfare of wildlife in the UK. And it is these organizations that do the lion's share of the work in terms of protecting wildlife, at present almost independently of government bodies. So there is scope for charitable organizations and government bodies that are concerned with the same issues to come together in unison and achieve fantastic results for the natural world. One such organization (that will remain nameless), in the UK, boasts a considerable number of members, most (if not all) of whom will make donations every year. While this organization does incredible work with the funds it gets, the fact cannot be ignored that its work takes a somewhat futile shape when the impact of domesticated cats on the ecosystem is, by them, overlooked. They suggest that cats have no effect on animal numbers. Pretty crazy when we consider the statistics. It's almost as if such organizations suffer from some kind of convoluted Stockholm syndrome. It is my belief that, due to the risk of funding coming into jeopardy, organizations are discouraged from suggesting to their members (many of whom will be cat owners) that a huge cause of the problems facing birds and other wildlife is their furry companion. After all, the funding available for wildlife conservation is already hard to come by as it is, especially when you have MPs dishing up public funds to themselves or their mates.

Namibia was the first country in Africa to enshrine environmental rights and justice in its constitution, placing these issues above party politics.[37] The people in positions of power over environmental matters – for example, the Under Secretary of State at the Department for Environment, Food and Rural Affairs – cannot be those who have a personal monetary investment in the land. This is a clear conflict of interest. Local communities should be given the power to oversee and manage their own ecological issues, through grassroots projects. Decision makers on the outdoors should be diverse boards of independent experts who have proven their dedication to their respective fields. If there is a pressing issue of environmental concern at hand, there should be a group of minds that come together and resolve the issues using their expertise and honest love for nature.

Landowners also need to be regulated and obliged to meet ecological criteria. 'We inherited it so it's ours and we can do what we want' isn't a good enough reason to own massive plots of land anymore. If you do not see to it that your land is increasing biodiversity and that you are extracting from it sustainably, you should be penalized at the very least. There is obviously a massive issue here regarding farmers and the service that they provide to the country, but I guess that that's a discussion for another book, since this one is focused on birds and other forms of wildlife.

At this point, let's get back to cats. An academic paper published in 2016 suggested that ethnicity and economic status have a part to play in pet ownership, particularly cats. Families of higher socio-economic standing were found to be more likely to own a cat or a dog.[38] Kids with step-relatives or single parents were also reported to have a far higher rate of cat ownership than children living with both of their biological parents. Also, the fewer children a family had, the more likely they were to own a pet. This further attests to the point that cats serve as an emotional buffer to human beings. The pets serve as a coping mechanism for emotional distress and feelings of anxiety.

Those stroking sessions with the cat on your lap really are good for your mental health, but they are a short-term fix. Love cannot be summoned as a matter of convenience; it is something that is worked out, forged and built over time by two totally mutual parties that grow an understanding for one another, like the house geckos in Sri Lanka. This is in contrast to 'house cats', which are bound to the confines of their human houses despite showing an obvious interest in the outside world every time the front door is opened. The study also showed that, when compared to people of African origin (who reside mostly in urban environments in the UK), white people were much more likely to own cats. So, we here establish that, in recent years, it is mostly lonely white people, of all classes, living in cities, who own cats. This is certainly the case in the Western world. I really do believe that this is a very telling fact. It offers us a brief insight into small cultural differences, which may have bigger implications than we ever thought.

Let's take a look at language and how cultures belonging to people of colour tend to use it to cultivate love in their lives and thus avoid the need to hold a captive animal in order to serve the innate human need for love, which we all have, no matter what our ethnicity. I can totally understand that there are socio-economic issues at play which may contribute to the demand for cats in the West, and there is no quick fix for this issue. I'm also aware that there are people who are physically incapable of getting outside and, for them, the companionship of a cat means a great deal. I'm just highlighting a *real* ecological threat in the hopes that some of us will begin to work towards solutions because, at the moment, there seem to be none.

In Sri Lanka, if you meet a stranger who is around your age, they are referred to as 'ayya/akki' or 'malli/nangi', which literally translate to 'big brother/sister' or 'little brother/sister'. That's if you speak Sinhalese, which is one of two major languages spoken on the island (the other is Tamil). Even to address strangers, we use terms that bring us closer together as a gesture of openness and trust in our fellow human beings. A stark contrast to the English language which has countless words to distance ourselves from one another ('I'm your second cousin, twice removed!'). In the Sinhala language, there is a word for cousin but it is really only ever used in formal writing and *never* spoken to address somebody. Everybody you meet is either your brother or sister, or your uncle or auntie. I think of my friends from Turkey and they have similar terms, such as 'abi', and even in 'hood' culture in the UK, there exist 'bruv', 'blud', 'cuz', which are all linguistic relics of a long-standing culture of forming communities through many means, daily language being one of them.

Now, I'm not saying that addressing people as 'brother' or 'sister' is going to instantly make you get rid of your cat or the urge to watch romcoms with a tub of ice cream. What I am saying, though, is that the use of language is a very accessible and easy way to try to begin cultivating love in your life. By indiscriminately bringing people closer to you in your use of language, you build a connectedness to all those you come across, and that will certainly begin to have an impact in this mostly loveless landscape. This is a great example of how, by solving an issue that affects mostly human beings (emotional discomfort), and thereby reducing the excessive number of predatory animals in our environment, the natural world can also benefit: both parties are one and the same.

What we can also see here is that the condition of living in cities is the perfect environment for loneliness and an incessant need to feel loved and to give love. We city-dwellers are all racing to get nowhere and allow the beauty of this planet to slip slowly from our view. We have such little time for meaningful exchanges with next-door neighbours, let alone family and loved ones, that we are forced to purchase (and rescue) animals to fulfil that totally human need within us. But perhaps we should question whether it is morally right for us to possess an animal for the sole reason of emotional support. Can we find other ways to fill that void within our lives? A way that perhaps doesn't contribute to the death of millions of animals each year.

Ollie done told you (see page 101); it takes a village to raise a child, b! A village is a community. A network of varying sources of love, perspectives and advice (good or bad). Where is your village, cat owners? Who are your ayyas and akkis? Nature is a fantastic way for you to get out and fulfil the loving part of yourself, which may have sought the companionship of an animal beforehand. Flock Together really did spark a global movement. By us being brave and fearlessly ourselves in a new space, we inspired others to do the same. So now, even if you aren't a person of colour, you can find an outdoors group that will fit your bill. Off the top of my head, I can think of outdoor groups for women, for Muslims, for Black women, and for many other marginalized groups who have popped up since Flock Together's first walk in 2020. We should all be celebrating each other, and right here is a wondrous celebration of all the community groups reclaiming nature for ourselves and finding strength, love and healing in community! Hopefully, you will be able to find one that suits you and join up.

One of my favourite things about Flock Together is that a lot of people come alone. This is humbling, not only because people feel comfortable enough to arrive with nobody, but also because *every single time* they come alone, they end the walk having made good friends, bonds and connections with our community. A community is a safe space, full of love. May you find yours, whether at Flock, or with another outdoor group, or just with a bunch of old friends in nature.

# BRING NATURE TO YOU

Putting up bird feeders in your home is a very accessible way to get some incredible views of the bird life around you. If you don't have a garden, there are feeders out there with suction cups which can stick onto any window in your house.

Put some feeders up and document all the birds you see by taking photos, or even starting your own bird species log. A few hours of watching the birds doing their thing every week will surely deliver some incredible benefits. You might even observe some behaviour among species that has never been recorded before!

# 6

# CREATIVE MENTORSHIP

**OLLIE**

Mentorship can come from anywhere; it is borderless. The friends from the communities I created became my mentors. Even though they were my peers, they still taught and guided me in different areas of my life. I have always believed mentorship isn't defined by one person; it should come from different perspectives. Our generation has had to learn how to adapt on the job, as we've been forced to work in rigid outdated systems with limited alternatives. Technology has put even more pressure on these old ways of working and, where we once demanded change, we now have the power to create and define our own worlds. But with all this I still strongly believe that progress needs to be cross-generational; we have to understand what has come before us in order not to repeat any mistakes. In the case of the Yao tribe referenced by Nadeem (see page 130), their traditions and skills have been passed down the generations for centuries. Without mentorship this would simply have been impossible. Their very survival depends on the highest level of knowledge-sharing.

In the West, Black children are told that to succeed in life we will have to work twice as hard as anyone else. When you grow up, you realize what that actually means. They weren't joking. According to the 2020 'The Race at Work: Black Voices Report', just 1.5 per cent of top management roles in the private sector are held by Black people, despite Black people making up more than 3 per cent of the population in England and Wales.[39] As a minority in the workplace, we are often forced into working at a different octane level. We overcompensate to prove our worth so we can reverse the years of being overlooked as a community. We can't make a mistake; we don't get second chances. Often marginalized, our minds are constantly on edge. Without support, this experience can create a whole world of damage to one's mental health and close relationships. Being held back at work or harassed because of your colour is crippling and can cause depression and anxiety. With the right network of friends, support system and mentorship, this feeling can be healed and talked through with those who have had the same experiences.

From the moment we wake up until the second we sleep, our conscious world is slammed with signs and sounds pulling us in different directions. Digital and physical interactions, every screen we see, book we read and film we watch influences our perception of the world. Good and bad information is processed throughout the day, in lessons, at work, relaxing at home; there is no escape from being bombarded with noise. Growing up, we learn behaviours and boundaries from parents, siblings, classmates and teachers, but a heavy amount of influence is drawn from our childhood heroes. These inspiring people are often found in popular music and sports. Sometimes it can be a case of our youthful attention being held by whoever shouts the loudest or whatever is trending on the playground that week, but somehow through the noise we tune into those with whom we find the most resemblance and common ground. As we mature, these interactions can create milestone moments that will have defining outcomes in our future.

Sports stardom dominated my teenage dreams, so I was drawn towards footballing heroes, among others who led me on my path. I was also drawn to Black Liberation in my mid- to late teens, which was probably down to the fact that my older brother put me onto Wu-Tang, 2Pac, NWA, and many other groups from that period. All these artists shared a common thread through their music – a thread that, at my impressionable age, I could relate to. I was rebellious, I struggled with authority, and nothing felt better than listening to DMX on max volume screaming every lyric. To this day I'm still surprised my parents let me do that, even on a Sunday morning when they were preparing to go to church. But without the influence of these rappers and political figures, I'm not sure what would have prepared me for the realities of the world that lay ahead of me. Today, it is a different story. The sources of influence are unlimited and unfiltered.

When I look back at my childhood, I wonder at how few films, books and television shows shed light and shared not only the struggles but also the joys and the many lived experiences of being Black. There were vanishingly few positive Black roles in the media. At the other end of the scale, there was the likes of *Tintin in the Congo*, where Black people were represented as ink-black, half-naked and big-lipped. What kind of impression does that give to a Black (or, indeed, white) child growing up? There are lasting effects of not seeing yourself mirrored in modern society. It leaves you with a subtle reminder that you are an outsider, invited to the party but left in the cold at the front door. It is only now through the fear of public shaming, and being cancelled, that society has been forced to even consider, let alone publicly celebrate, the heroes of our Black heritage. There is hope, the baton is firmly in our hand, and it is down to us to keep moving forward with this positive change.

This was one of the main reasons why we launched the Flock Together Academy in 2021. Both myself and Nadeem relied on youth clubs when we were young, and as adults we have both worked within our communities on youth-focused initiatives. It didn't just make sense to open up Flock to a younger generation; it was our duty. We both lived in Hackney, in a part of London that had seen some of the biggest cuts to youth services in the entire country. There was no way we could sit back and not contribute to a solution in some way. I remember the first few sessions of the Academy we did, and how nervous and apprehensive the young people were when they arrived. But, once they could see themselves in us, they opened up. If you mixed the Chuckle Brothers with Will Smith and Martin Lawrence from *Bad Boys*, then you might have a picture of our teaching style. All the activities centred around helping these young people see the benefits of having a connection to nature, but we were conscious to deliver these lessons with excitement and innovation.

When we are young, our brains are litmus paper, absorbing every detail we encounter. In those early years we have a powerful imagination, we are willing to learn through play and we are much more open to new experiences that could lead to fruitful prospects and confidence, but the opportunities to live out those dreams are limited or non-existent for those less privileged. With the right direction, from the right role models, these aspirations can be identified early and realized. And remember, you need not look far. If you are a second- or third-generation person of colour reading this, then potentially every single member of your family – one of your great-grandmothers, grandfathers, aunties and uncles – is a hero.

The waves of immigration throughout the generations must be remembered. Those brave souls who took that leap of faith to start a new life, from one country to another, are the epitome of heroic. In our current times – filled with questions on race and class – social solitude can be a personal prison, without somewhere to go to feel safe and secure. The mind can wander without the grounding influence of someone to trust and talk to openly. We people of colour have a shared history with common interests, and it is our responsibility to pass down the knowledge learned from our journey on to the next generation. The baton needs to keep moving forward.

Back in Coventry, my reputation for pulling together different crowds had grown rapidly, and TrampsInPrada had a constant stream of colourful kids through the shop doors. I enjoyed my new-found independence and status, I learned on my feet during buying trips to London for vintage clothes, and my articles dissecting brands on the BNTL website were receiving praise from the creative industries. Learning how to build these communities was the foundation of everything I have ever achieved. With all the success I was experiencing at home, my gut, my inner compass, was drawing me closer to London life. By 22 I had moved to the capital, convinced my future lay in the Big Smoke. I had enough money to last me about four months, and by chance there was a spare room in a friend's dormitory. It was now down to me to make something happen.

I had no guidance in making this decision. If I had sought counsel, I would probably have been called insane and my big city dreams would have been dashed. With no job, very little money and only a temporary roof over my head, on paper I was destined for disaster. Thankfully, the creative community took me in. We had built real friendships, purely born from our digital relationships, and supported each other's work since the days of online forums. When I started meeting up with them in London, it was as if we had been close friends for years. We were an instant family. A multiracial, inclusive and influential family made up of artists, musicians, designers and all-round doers. My friendship with them helped me dive head first into the London social scene. Aligning yourself with those who subconsciously push you forward is an important foundation for success. There is a great impact in who you choose to surround yourself with on a daily basis. Within a few months of being in the right place at the right time, I started to receive invitations from the gatekeepers of the creative industry.

Whenever my workload and responsibilities increased, I used nature as a way of escaping the pressures of the office. In the evening after work or early in the morning, I would regularly go on long walks with my phone on silent to clear my head. Looking back, it was so important for me to do those things to survive in Babylon. I came with the understanding that this is the rat race, London can swallow you up and spit you out, so I needed nature as my one constant; my anchor when the seas got rough. When you're out in nature, the environment grounds you and reminds you of the bigger picture; it puts things into perspective when you feel you might be losing your way.

After less than a year in London, my insightful trend forecasting and growing following caught the attention of an international advertising agency. Before I knew it, I was in a boardroom being headhunted for a large role on a social impact campaign for children's charity Barnardo's. This was the first official step of my career specializing in the empowerment of individuals and communities. As a child, I had to fight to be heard, fight to be accepted and fight to be understood. With that being my introduction to society, I knew no other way, so when I approached my working career, that fight was still alive and kicking within me to be a voice to the voiceless. I had been let down by education, religion, society – I was now being embraced by my peers.

When I was brought into a big advertising agency as a freelancer, I found myself one of only two non-white faces in the office. Naively unaware at the time, I wasn't invited into those boardrooms just because I possessed the 'cool cultured guy' card, but because I had a unique perspective that the industry could never grasp and still struggles with today.

In this wide expansive glass office there was an Asian co-worker who had a reputation for being *the best* – he was so good at his job, it made other colleagues anxious. I admired him for his head-down work ethic and enviable results. Plus, we were the only two people of colour in the whole office at the time so, by default, we became friends. At the end of the successful campaign, we all went our separate ways. I tried to get in contact with him, but he ignored my email. There was no reply to my follow-up a few weeks later either. I thought that, as fellow people of colour, we would be able to connect on a couple of levels, especially considering our mutual career paths. My presumption was that he would have been through the same struggles and off-key experiences at the water cooler as I had. Then it dawned on me – not everyone is willing to help. The workplace is a competitive environment; it is not ingrained in us all to support each other.

There were moments when it was lonely being the only person of colour in the room, but it was also incredibly powerful. Escaping into nature was the only place where there were no demands on me at all. Being outside was an environment where I felt secure, and it gave me an opportunity to think freely and develop ideas for the boardroom. I found that the more I spoke, the more the people around me listened. It was essential for the companies I worked with to appeal to all demographics. My experience as a Black man ensured I had a different perspective on incoming projects. My alternative views could not be ignored if the companies hoped to deliver successful campaigns. Not all agencies cared and, unfortunately, the industry does do a good job of ignoring these experiences still to this day. Forced into a situation where I had to trust my gut, I had no one to turn to who I felt understood me or my situation as a Black person in advertising. I had no choice but to use my intuition and become my own mentor.

The generation before mine was all about scarcity. They existed in a time where only a small number of people of colour could be found in particular careers. In some industries, African or Caribbean people were a rarity right up until the late 1990s. The struggle was real for our brothers and sisters back then. Things haven't changed much today, with 78 per cent of young Black respondents to a survey reporting hearing and witnessing racist language in the workplace.[40] Being the token Black person in the office opened the door to hushed racist remarks, awkward innuendos and workplace discrimination. HR can't save you when they're laughing and making jokes too. The era of the black square taught us this, when brands were quick to post their support for the Black community with these public statements, but then the staff followed with even more public stories of how they continue to mistreat their Black members of staff. In many cases, the HR team were the ones who took the bullet, rightfully so, but heads need to roll from the board as well.

A few years into my career, in another huge agency, I discovered that I shared my birthday with the boss of the company. They made a huge song and dance about it on the day for him, going all out with the presentation of cake and presents, with all the staff gathered in the communal area. After the tiered cake for the big boss arrived, a huddled group of staff members turned to me and said, 'Don't worry, we haven't forgotten about you...' And then I was presented with a bowl of chicken wings lit by birthday candles.

Yes, I really wanted the ground to swallow me up, but instead I had to laugh along with everyone else. Shit like this happens to us on the daily. We brush it off, not making a fuss, and get on with our day. There is an assumed narrative: our identity is put on trial at school, at work and in social spaces at every turn. We learn to accept that this treatment is a part of navigating living in the West. We are taught to laugh off problematic experiences just to survive. It is soul-crushing. Nature and its space for healing helps you overcome these negative experiences, because you can really focus on yourself. That freedom gives you space to realize what you need.

My Asian colleague from my old company must have learned to keep quiet early on, stayed away from the pack and let his results do the talking. The effect of long-term competition, inequality and an exclusionary office culture may have led him to adopt an 'every man for himself' mentality. Perhaps he felt he was alone, and in that swell of solitude he was too far gone to realize when someone was reaching out. Or maybe he already had his support network, but didn't think to include another brother who needed guidance. The workplace doesn't necessarily feel like a safe space for speaking out when you're dealing with people who are questioning your right to even be there. 'Just keep your head down and try to make it through the project.'

It's clear that having a network to lean on is crucial, but how hard is it to build networks when the working world is full of managers who like to hire people who remind them of their younger selves? You look around you in any of these offices and boardrooms, and so many people share a similar story. They grew up comfortably, excelled in school, got good grades at A level, felt like they lived a little by moving to a city for university, where they had your typical student experience. Maybe they had a gap year somewhere 'exotic', came back and decided London was the place for them. All this is perfectly fine, but here's where I get a little bit tetchy. A lot of these types of people then either get supported by their parents or family friends to intern for free, or if they're extra-lucky they get to enter places like creative industries through the back door without the 'relevant' experience. At the same time, these brands and agencies are hand-picking students that fit the mould of their set-up; this way they're easy to manage. The problem we're then left with is there's no new thinking: everyone through the door has had the same kind of experience, has got the same story to tell, is happy to play it safe and tick the box, and there's no one willing or able to challenge outdated ways of working. This leads to one-dimensional work that tends to only speak to a specific set of people, which results in leaving lots of communities disenfranchised.

If having a network is crucial for getting ahead, then a Black network will admittedly be just as culpable as the white one I have just described. But if this is the best way of achieving a level playing field, then we have to accept that, for the time being at least, two wrongs can make a right.

The pressures to support each other can also be too much when you have a job to do. I understand that, and not everyone has the personality to kick down doors. Another scenario that I remember, which shows how complex this space is for us, was when I was at another big agency. A couple of years into my time there, I was overjoyed to see a Black lady in her mid-thirties walk through the door. As one of the first ever Black staff members the company had employed, I went to welcome her and introduce myself as a friendly face she could trust. Clearly institutionalized, she embarrassingly ignored my greeting. Just as my Asian colleague had learned years before, my new older Black female co-worker was employing the same tactics for survival on the office floor. I believe this mindset has been displayed by people of colour in most industries from generation to generation. It is our time to break these problematic traditions and understand it's our duty to be there for our skinfolk.

We are the next generation; we are made differently, cut from a different fabric. We have been born into a more open-minded era of time, and we genuinely care about each other, the environment and human rights. We are more likely to stick together and support one another as a group – unlike previous generations, where the premise of climbing up the corporate ladder seems to have been a selfish single-player game. Industries complain about the lack of Black creatives, but where is the care and support when you hire them? We are just thrown into the lion's den, lost in the system. Black women are told their hair is 'unprofessional'. White colleagues are insensitive to the trauma caused by seeing yet another news cycle filled with images of the violent death of a Black man. Instead of addressing discriminatory behaviour through staff training programmes, companies expect new Black hires to do the work of advocating for themselves.

It's on us to be there for one another. We have got to take it out of the group chat and unite. There is solidarity in numbers: by taking the time to learn about each other's intersectionality, we learn more about ourselves. When you combine these differing world views for a common goal, that's when magic happens. With an open mind we can be a positive influence on each other, sharing personal experiences that could support someone who has never had access to that alternative view. Mixing opinions to allow for experimentation: it's in that where innovation can be born. If these skills are not taught at school, then we must try to teach

one another. If there is disparity in the workplace, then we must become the protectors of the support system.

A pivotal moment for me in understanding the strength in bringing people with different perspectives together came when I was invited to a retreat hosted by some philosophers in 2018. In attendance were around twenty of us, ranging from futurists and professors to architects and climate and ecological experts. I was as shocked as anyone to be invited to share the weekend with these brains. Our challenge was to see 'short-termism' as an existential crisis and to ask the question: how can we look beyond our current view of the future and go further? When we do that, what can we learn that we can bring into the present, so we feel and act with more responsibility? Bringing art and culture into the conversation around saving our planet, the weekend was centred around a schedule of workshops that looked at the history of the universe, death meditation (yep, that's really a thing), intergenerational thinking through different indigenous cultures, empathy to stretch our ability to care, and even fire pit rituals. It was a truly liberating experience, with so much learning to be had. I came away and, consciously and subconsciously, how I approached my work changed for good. Without the shackles of rigid systems, we had all been free at the retreat to explore without limits. We not only borrowed from the past, but we also borrowed from each other. At the start, I questioned if I had the experience to be a part of this group, but by the end I knew how important my perspective was. Not only was I the only Black person in attendance, but also the perspective and understanding around communities that I could bring to the table were as valuable as anything shared across the weekend.

Thanks to a wide variety of online resources, alternative learning has been on the rise for the past decade. Young people trust YouTube over their parents and teachers. The current educational system has tunnel vision, full of Eurocentrism in stuffy rooms using old techniques. The premise of school and education needs redefining. Agencies and collectives are the new educators, sharing knowledge and empowerment. Talent is distributed evenly, but opportunity is not. This is the reason why I have the drive to create spaces for people who look like me, think like me and are less fortunate than I have been. The hurdles I have overcome to have my voice heard, the years of hard work, will not be wasted. I cannot ignore the need to pass on the knowledge I have learned.

At the start of your career, you are given the message that, in order to climb up the corporate ladder, you must dress the part, fall in line and leave your individuality at the door. Our only option is to try to walk in others' shoes, but after a few steps you quickly realize the shoe doesn't fit and never will. In fact, the shoe was never meant for you. But just because a system or method has been performed a particular way for decades does not mean a new technique can't rise up and completely change the game. That is what it felt like for me working in advertising. I did everything in my power to be the best I could be. I not only survived in an all-white environment, but I managed to thrive.

Exhausted from working in advertising agencies that didn't feel like home, however, I decided to do something about it, break the mould and create my own. Taking all my skills, fears and insecurities, I launched my first agency, Superimpose, that would go on to become globally recognized and award-winning. To do that, my reliance on nature for ideation was fundamental. The woods gave me everything I needed for inspiration. As an agency we wanted to brazenly challenge how the industry worked. We thought of ourselves as a New World creative offering, challenging brands to go further. We aimed to push the limits of experience and spark meaningful conversation in our campaigns. I wanted to kick down the doors of the dinosaurs that ran the show and leave a lasting impression on the advertising world. Not just gunning for the campaign credit or landing the big fish brands, we wanted to do things differently and open the doors for others to do the same. Without being pigeonholed, we were independent, culturally rooted and globally active. The work we produced for projects tested boundaries from the very beginning and was deliberately provocative. Never satisfied with creating simple work for our clients, we went above and beyond to prove that there were innovative ways and means in the creative process. We flourished outside the normal realms of the industry in order to deliver impressive and memorable results.

Within a few years, our hard work and risk paid off: we became a leading global agency. For Adidas we relaunched their biggest-selling 'Adidas Originals' trainer ever, the 'Stan Smith', alongside campaigns for Donald Glover, Pusha T and Stormzy. We were asked to guide the art direction of Christopher Bailey's final collection for Burberry, as well as the repositioning and creative direction for Tommy Hilfiger's 'Hilfiger Collection'. Outside of brands, we created a national campaign around Brexit that saw me work with the campaign officer for Barack Obama and go on Sky News talking politics. We deliberately employed outsiders and free thinkers who cared. By 2016 I had built a culture in my company to a place I could proudly call home. I had the glass office in the sky in London, Los Angeles and New York, won the awards and became that household name within the industry. I did it all by following my life's work of empowering individuals and communities.

We need to remove the gatekeepers – the people who have kept us out of industries for all these years; the fat cats and middle management who are scared of losing their positions, fearful of what change could mean for their future. There are no more gods. There is a new era upon us, and the industries are experiencing a renaissance. The dinosaurs are on the verge of extinction again. They now have a duty to uphold their corporate responsibilities to all employees with legal codes and staff handbooks. Nowadays there is public opinion and social media holding them to account; we are one step closer, but the fight is not over yet. There is power in the people. We just need to realize and unleash it as one.

People are going to tell you it's hard, that it's impossible to win in a white person's world. Others will say 'that's just the way it is'. They are wrong. The world has completely changed, we are in a state of evolution and there are no more rules. There are opportunities everywhere, and they are yours for the taking. We need to demystify industries. We can be the shepherd steering the next flock to safety. We can show the next generation new roads into the game, and teach them how to create an economy within their own industry, or how to convert a side hustle into a long-term career. To succeed you need to have the self-confidence to believe you can overcome anything. These businesses need you more than you need them. You set the rules. For these industries to survive in the future they need your ideas.

At the start of my career, being allowed to speak and be heard in boardrooms changed the trajectory of my path. As my experience grew further, I was able to give my opinions with conviction and without fear. That taught me to always believe in younger employees, full of raw energy and pure ideas. Just as I had the chance in the early days of my career, in my company I actively put young people in the boardroom. At first, they are shy to talk up but after a few weeks there is no fear in speaking openly. I enjoy filling people with confidence and seeing a young staff member blossom. And when they speak with honesty, we all win.

Running an agency isn't all plain sailing. The pressure was, and still is, intense: I came close to breaking point on many occasions, but somehow managed to survive it. The common denominator throughout was nature. If only more people could experience these benefits from a young age. There is a link between creativity and green spaces. I truly felt like any task was possible when walking through the trees. Nature brought calm to my chaos, nature brought peace to my mind and nature showed me what was really worth fighting for. Without nature I would never have had that space for discovery. I could only see the bigger picture by allowing myself the space to think without restraints or distraction.

Flock Together is made up of over one hundred young professionals across a variety of industries. Our members include lawyers, directors, musicians, journalists, doctors, artists, and much more. Many of these individuals have fought hard for success within their careers. We believe the experience our members have gained is a valuable insight to be shared with the next generation of POC creatives. We have a rare culture of positivity in the Flock. Usually in any 'networking' events there's a level of competition surrounding introductions, with peppered egotism, but at Flock Together we are genuinely present to support each other entirely. We are a flock, not a rat race. We move forward as a collective.

Working with young people who are finishing school or nearing adulthood, Flock Together gives support in that crucial next step. Through mentorship we break the traditional 'career advice' and deliver our own message of community through our relatable members. We will not be exploited, we are united. In 2021, we launched the Flock Together Academy for under-supported children, with a variety of nature activities. Among the flag-making, breathwork and birdwatching, we provide the mentorship for children who need it most, supplying that missing link wherever that may be. Most importantly, these sessions are delivered by people who the children can relate to. Who knows what these young people can go on to achieve if we give them the confidence at this crucial moment?

In the conversation of conservation, for decades we have been seeing the same tactics, from the same people, about the climate crisis. We are past the point of no return, so it is crucial that we start hearing from new voices – and not just gimmicks. Only then, through experimentation, can we see much-needed innovation. I believe anything is possible. We are trying to unlock the power, potential and influence of *the* most creative demographic, from musicians and film-makers to fashion influencers and the creators of TikTok's most viral dances – the Black community. With Flock we are bringing new thinking to that space, hoping to unlock minds and start to develop the creative problem-solvers who are going to go on to change the world. Flock Together is that safe space I wish I'd had when I was a child. A place I could seek validation, find life guidance and have my questions on race and equality answered. It is our home from home, a breeding ground for a better future.

# MAP YOUR MOMENTS IN NATURE

Write down here five memories involving nature. Did your friend once fall in a river? Did a robin land on your lap? Did your dog chase the leaves blowing in the wind?

No matter how serious or funny, write down any nature-related memories here. Use them as a reference to times when you were connected to the Earth and just how important those feelings and connections are to you. Do you miss it when you're not in nature?

If you can't think of five memories right now, it's cool. There's always tomorrow.

# CONCLUSION

## OLLIE & NADEEM

The end of a journey is beautiful because it ever so subtly implies the beginning of the next one. As we write the closing of this book, we can't help but feel that the timing is perfect, in that our outdoors movement is moving simultaneously to its next phase. To look to the future, Flock Together will remain ambitious in its endeavours. The truth is that we have smashed all our initial objectives out of the park, and now we have a taste for high-level achievement and progress for our organization and, in turn, our entire global community. The past two years have been eye-opening and useful in bringing our community's plight to the forefront of not only mainstream media outlets, but also the minds of our community itself. As we look to the future, our focus is on the joy and prosperity of our people. Smiles, style, positive impact and greenery are what lie ahead.

We have big creative energy and want our legacy to be everlasting. None of our children or people-dem should feel out of place, figuratively or literally, and by working together as a collective, we can diversify our approach to solving this problem. This can apply across the board and not just in the natural world. Creativity is what drives not only our society forward but the natural world too. Innovation (or evolution) is what allows a species to outcompete another, or even fellow members within its own species. This sounds harsh at first, but it actually leads into something rather significant and beautiful. Take, for example, the peppered moth (*Biston betularia*). This common moth species gets its name from its white and black speckled appearance. It is thought that its pattern would camouflage it against rocks or trees with mosses or fungi for it to blend in with. Pre-1811 this was the only known colouration of this moth species; however, the Industrial Revolution was booming at the time, meaning environments were becoming darker and duller in colour, not least because of the copious amounts of soot filling the air and settling on the surrounding surfaces. Such a state of affairs would then leave this pale-coloured moth exposed in any urban area, like chalk on a blackboard. So nature did with this hardship what it tends to do with any difficult situation thrown at it; it pushed for evolution in its creation. It began to search in genetics, the very core of a being, to find solutions that would ensure the survival of its figurative child.

By 1848, 98 per cent of all peppered moths collected in a field study were darker than the 'original' colour of the peppered moth. This was in Manchester, a massively industrial city at the time.

What this showed was that even though the paler coloured moths were, sadly, more likely to have been preyed on and killed, they did make space for the darker coloured mutants to survive. Eventually the mutated moths were quickly passing on their genes and a new population with much better survival tools was beginning to emerge. Similarly, Flock Together and many groups like us within our community are beginning to innovate and evolve, with previous generations having sacrificed so much in order for us to be where we are today.

It is a promising state of affairs for the natural world if our community begins to play a bigger role in what goes on in it. We are nature and its children simultaneously. We face the hardship put upon us by the world and, in the face of it all, we are still able to provide the VIBESSSSSSS that the entire world rocks to until this day. We are leaders in fashion, sport, music and the arts, as if unfazed by the many reasons we have to despair. It is time now that we become a substantial influence on the natural world and restore the bond between ourselves and the source of our energy and joy: our creator, Mother Nature. She is free to access and grants us freedom in her ever-giving grace! We have found our haven in nature, and it is there that we can regroup and mobilize so that future generations, the beautiful young minds of tomorrow, will have nature as a reference point for the big ideas they are bound to produce.

# NOTES

1 Jake Stuart Veasy, 'Can Zoos Ever Be Big Enough for Large Wild Animals? A Review Using an Expert Panel Assessment of the Psychological Priorities of the Amur Tiger (*Panthera tigris altaica*) as a Model Species', *Animals*, 10 (9), August 2020: 1536.

2 Valentina Di Stasio and Anthony Heath, 'Are Employers in Britain Discriminating against Ethnic Minorities?', GEMM Project, Centre for Social Investigation, Nuffield College, Oxford University, 18 January 2019.

3 Christine Grandy, 'How "The Black and White Minstrel Show" Spent 20 Years on the BBC', British Academy, 24 January 2019.

4 See Gus John, 'Cy Grant Obituary', *The Guardian*, 17 February 2010.

5 Candice Williams, 'Jordan Peele On Why He Likely Won't Cast White Male Lead: "I've Seen That Movie"', ABC News, 27 March 2019.

6 See Ella Glover, 'Can Going for a Walk Every Day Really Change Your Life?', *Metro*, 26 December 2021.

7 See Haroon Siddique, 'New Bill Quietly Gives Powers to Remove British Citizenship Without Notice', *The Guardian*, 17 November 2021. Frances Webber, vice-chair of the Institute of Race Relations, is quoted in the article as noting: 'This

amendment sends the message that certain citizens, despite being born and brought up in the UK and having no other home, remain migrants in this country. Their citizenship, and therefore all their rights, are precarious and contingent.'

8   Office for National Statistics, 'Ethnicity and National Identity in England and Wales: 2011', 11 December 2012.

9   See 'Was Robert Baden-Powell a Supporter of Hitler?', BBC News, 11 June 2020.

10  See Annabel Rose, 'How Scouts is Becoming Anti-racist', www.scouts.org.uk/news, 24 August 2020.

11  See Ashley John-Baptiste, 'The Black Children Wrongly Sent to "Special" Schools in the 1970s', BBC News, 20 May 2021.

12  'The Report of the Committee of Inquiry into the Education of Children from Ethnic Minority Groups' (chairman Lord Swann FRSE), March 1985.

13  Lilla Watson, quoted in Dr Nicole Evans, Faybra Hemphill, Daisy Han and Katie Kitchens, 'Our Liberation is Bound Together', Embracing Equity, 1 June 2020.

14  See, for example, Matt Williams, 'A Universe of 10 Dimensions', Phys.org, 11 December 2014.

15  Claire N. Spottiswoode, Keith S. Begg and Colleen M. Begg, 'Reciprocal Signaling in Honeyguide-Human Mutualism', *Science*, 353 (6297), 22 July 2016: 387–9.

16  Government Office for Science, 'Trend Deck 2021: Urbanisation', www.gov.uk, 28 June 2021.

17  'Saving Species: Red Squirrels', The Wildlife Trusts, n.d.

18  'History of Control: Actively Promoting the Humane Cull-

ing of Grey Squirrels', Grey Squirrel Control, n.d.

19  Anna Lisa Signorile et al, 'Mixture or Mosaic? Genetic Patterns in UK Grey Squirrels Support a Human-Mediated "Long-Jump" Invasion Mechanism', *Diversity and Distributions*, 22 (5), May 2016: 566–77.

20  Rural Payments Agency and Natural England, 'Squirrel Control and Management', www.gov.uk, 8 February 2022.

21  https://www.englefieldestate.co.uk/the-estate

22  See Guy Shrubsole, *Who Owns England? How We Lost Our Green and Pleasant Land, and How to Take It Back*, London: William Collins, 2019.

23  Journalist George Monbiot covers this topic extensively and does not shy away from pointing the finger at the British government, right down to naming individuals. His admirable writing has informed much of my opinion on the matter of the grey squirrel.

24  See, for example, Jack Peat, 'UK Taxpayers were Paying Compensation to Slave Traders until 2015', *The London Economic,* 11 June 2020.]

25  See, for example, 'Addressing our Histories of Colonialism and Historic Slavery', National Trust, September 2020.

26  Jonathan Leake and Hannah Summers, 'Wildlife Minister Chops Down his Trees', *The Times*, 9 December 2012.

27  George Monbiot, 'Richard Benyon, the Minister Destroying What He is Paid to Protect', *The Guardian*, 20 April 2012.

28  Sena S. De Silva and Giovanni M. Turchini, 'Towards Understanding the Impacts of the Pet Food Industry on World Fish

and Seafood Supplies', *Journal of Agricultural and Environmental Ethics*, 21, 10 July 2008: 459–67.

29  See Rebecca L. Thomas, Philip J. Baker and Mark D. E. Fellowes, 'Ranging Characteristics of the Domestic Cat (*Felis catus*) in an Urban Environment', *Urban Ecosystems*, 17 (4), April 2014: 911–21.

30  'The Cat Watch Project', Cats Protection, 29 October 2021.

31  Nicole Cosgrove, '12 UK Animal Shelter Statistics & Facts to Know in 2022: Benefits, Facts & More', Pet Keen, 21 March 2022.

32  See, for example, David Zax, 'A Brief History of House Cats', *Smithsonian Magazine*, 30 June 2007, and Press Association, 'Long Tail: Dogs May Have Lived With Humans for 30,000 Years', *The Guardian*, 21 May 2015.

33  'How Many Birds do Cats Kill?', RSPB (Royal Society for the Protection of Birds), n.d.

34  Arie Trouwborst and Han Somsen, 'Domestic Cats (*Felis catus*) and European Nature Conservation Law – Applying the EU Birds and Habitats Directives to a Significant but Neglected Threat to Wildlife', *Journal of Environmental Law*, 32 (3), November 2020: 391–415.

35  See Graham Readfearn, 'Australian Wildlife 20 Times More Likely to Encounter Deadly Feral Cats Than Native Predators', *The Guardian*, 6 January 2021.

36  Anthony Ham, 'Australia's Cats Kill Two Billion Animals Annually. Here's How the Government is Responding to the Crisis', *Smithsonian Magazine*, 17 March 2021.

37  www.namibiaembassyusa.org/sites/default/files/state-
    ments/Environmental Laws of Namibia (1).pdf

38  Ferran Marsa-Sambola et al, 'Sociodemographics of Pet Own-
    ership among Adolescents in Great Britain: Findings from
    the HBSC Study in England, Scotland, and Wales', *Anthro-
    zoös*, 29 (4), December 2016: 559–80.

39  'The Race at Work: Black Voices Report', Business in the
    Community, 2020: 5.

40  'Young and Black: The Young Black Experience of Institution-
    al Racism in the UK', YMCA, October 2020: 7.

# ABOUT THE AUTHORS

Ollie Olanipekun is a Creative Director, based in North-east London. He is the founder of award-winning creative agency Futurimpose and has social responsibility at the core of his work. Empowering individuals and communities throughout his career, Ollie is committed to supporting marginalized groups as well as building smoother pathways into the creative industries for the next generation of 'non-traditional' creatives.

Nadeem Perera is a sports coach and activist, based in Bristol. A self-taught birdwatcher for over a decade, he has acquired expert knowledge of birds, other wildlife and the great outdoors in rural England. He has found ways to connect this experience with communities of all ages through his work in youth football and other sports.

Founded by Ollie Olanipekun and Nadeem Perera in summer 2020, Flock Together is the UK's first birdwatching collective for people of colour. Flock Together has been highlighted in numerous articles in the press, including *Vogue*, *The Times*, *Time Out* and *The Telegraph*, and has been filmed and featured in an ongoing series for *The One Show*. Flock Together has also partnered with various high-profile brands, including Gucci, The North Face, the RSPB and the National Trust.